A Message from
CEO Concern Worldwide

Anyone who picks up this book will know that on 12 January 2010 an earthquake struck the Haitian capital Port-au-Prince and shattered the lives of its inhabitants. More than 220,000 people died and two million were left homeless.

Concern Worldwide launched an immediate response to help those most affected by the earthquake. We raised €8.75 million from the Irish public and thanks to their generosity Concern's assistance in rebuilding lives is continuing.

It is truly remarkable that in the middle of a period of financial stress, people had the willingness and, indeed, the bravery to dig deep into their pockets to help the Haitian people.

This book is an example of one of hundreds of individual fundraising projects that sprang up around the country after the disaster, and displays the creativity that exists in Ireland, as well as our solidarity with those less fortunate than us.

Each story in this book, whether happy, sad, funny or poignant, acts as a vote of hope and confidence in the Haitian people. Concern has worked in Haiti since 1994 and in the first six months following the disaster, we reached more than 225,000 people, providing shelter, sanitation services, nutrition services, cash-for-work programmes and a host of other activities. We are committed to the country's future. We will continue our work for as long at it takes. Concern is able to do this because of your donations.

Thank you again for your extraordinary generosity.

A Pint and a Haircut

A Message from SoftCo,
Proud Sponsors of *A Pint and a Haircut*

SoftCo are delighted to sponsor *A Pint and a Haircut: True Irish Stories* in aid of Concern's Haiti Fund. The earthquake that struck Haiti's capital on 12 January 2010 had devastating effects and we hope that the proceeds of this book will help in some small way to improve the lives of those affected. SoftCo is an international software company, founded and headquartered in Ireland since 1990 and Garret has been an important part of our team for eleven years. We are extremely proud of all his hard work on behalf of those who suffered in Haiti.

A Pint and a Haircut
True Irish Stories

Edited by Garret Pearse

LONDUBH BOOKS

First published in 2010 by

Londubh Books

18 Casimir Avenue, Harold's Cross, Dublin 6w, Ireland

www.londubh.ie

1 3 5 4 2

Cover by Jon Bond; cover illustration courtesy of Liam Daly, www.bicyclistic.com

Origination by Londubh Books

Printed in Ireland by ColourBooks, Baldoyle Industrial Estate, Dublin 13

ISBN: 978-1-907535-16-1

Copyright © the contributors 2010

'The Prisoner's Dilemma' by John Butler was first published in *The Irish Times*

The contributors have asserted their moral rights.

Acknowledgements

I was reading a book called *True Tales of American Lives* when I first heard the news of the earthquake in Haiti. The book is a compilation of stories sent to author Paul Auster as part of his weekly programme on National Public Radio. The criterion for inclusion was simple – the story could be about anything as long as it was true. This suggested to me the idea of compiling stories as a means of raising funds for Concern's relief work in Haiti. The only further criterion I added was that the stories must relate to Ireland in some way, however vague. A website was set up and a chain email pleading for contributions was dispatched. Incredibly, my pleas were answered – by regular writers, aspiring writers and many who had never sat down and written a story in their lives before but who felt moved to do so in aid of Haiti. Over the course of three months, I received more than 140 stories. This book is a selection of about seventy of these stories.

A *Pint and a Haircut* is the result of the contributions, help and support of countless people to whom I am eternally grateful:

My wife and de facto assistant editor Jane, my children Charlie and Hannah and my mother, Judy, for all their love and support throughout this project and beyond.

Sarah Webb and Des Cox for their invaluable help and advice.

Vanessa O'Loughlin of Inkwell writers, Willie O'Reilly and Matt Cooper of Today FM and Eimear Rigby of Concern.

Jim Coffey and Susan Spence and all at SoftCo for their generosity, without which this book might never have seen the light of day.

Jon Bond for his cover design.

Liam Daly for kindly permitting the use of his wonderful painting on the cover.

All the newspapers and radio stations who helped to publicise the project.

Jo O'Donoghue and Hugh O'Donoghue of Londubh Books for their help, advice and patience.

All those who submitted a story. I just wish we could have fitted them all in.

There are many other people who have helped, some in ways of which I'm not even aware, but to all of you I say thank you.

I'm hoping to bring out a second volume of stories so if you have your own true Irish story, you can send it to trueirishstories@gmail.com. See www.trueirishstories.com for more details.

Garret Pearse, September 2010

Contents

Foreword	*Matt Cooper*	13
Providence	*Michael Owens*	15
A Tribute to the Large Family	*Mary Lynch*	17
The Waterford Connection	*Pat Hanrahan*	21
Our Lady of Dublin	*Nuala Ní Chonchúir*	24
Hurry Home	*Linda Gillett*	26
Firsts	*Jody Collins*	29
A Pint and a Haircut	*James Smith*	31
Silas	*Paul Reidy*	33
The Chantypoe Champion	*Jack O'Donnell*	37
Speech! Speech!	*Ian O'Malley*	39
The Prisoner's Dilemma	*John Butler*	44
World Peace	*Siobhán Donohue*	47
Froggy	*Maura Melia*	49
Michael and Eileen	*Andrew Shiels*	53
Shallow Grave	*Mary Sheehan*	56
Dis-ease With It Come Darkness and Peace	*Mary Clare O'Brien* *Emer Davis*	60 64
A Marriage of Inconvenience	*Quentin Fottrell*	67
Nanny to the Rescue	*Mary Dunne*	72
Bean Sídhe	*Pól Mac Reannacháin*	74
Lost in Translation	*Jim Gargan*	77
A Tale, a Tale	*Vanessa Delaney*	82
Memories of my Father	*Sarah Robertson*	85

The Making of an Imaginary Friend	*Sylvia Petter*	86
A Dublin Sunday	*Elizabeth Brickley*	88
Golden Goose Bay	*Clare O'Beara*	90
Firedance	*Barry Devlin*	93
Summer Mania	*Mary Mullen*	95
Surgical Wonderland	*Deirdre Brennan*	98
Higher, Stronger, Faster	*Neville Cox*	104
First Love	*Thady Dunne*	108
Epiphany	*Liz Quinn-Einstein*	111
The Beerosphere	*Cormac Eklof*	114
Gift of Garrykennedy	*Kevin Wells*	118
An Irish Exile	*Anne O'Curry*	121
Things Disappear	*Fred Johnston*	124
Mind Yourself	*Fiona Deverell*	128
Fender Bender	*John Piggott*	135
Reluctant Bachelors	*Mary McCombs*	137
The Emigrant Boat	*Eddie Walsh*	140
Move Over, Soccer Mom, I'm a GAA Ma!	*Barbara Scully*	141
A Kansas City Phone Call to an Irish Mother	*Liam Daly*	144
Belfast Brick	*Francesca Walsh*	148
Good Grief	*Lyn Duff*	150
All Set for D-Day	*Kathy McDevitt*	153
Tide-Turning	*Adrienne Troy*	157
The Other Side	*S. O'Dwyer*	160
Search for a School Motto	*Alan Cox*	166
The Liar	*Kathryn Crowley*	168
Irish Resourcefulness – with A Sting in the Tail	*Jerry Purcell*	170
Football Confession	*Conal Brennan*	172
The Family Shop	*Ethel Corduff*	173

The Door	*Majella Reid*	175
A Healing Sting	*Norman Fitzgerald*	179
Under the Clock at Clery's	*Maria Duffy*	182
How to Skin the Rabbit Man	*Lawrence Cloake*	185
Miss Rochford	*Gerry McDonnell*	187
Dog, Lost	*Fiona Tierney*	189
The Pig-Killing Hat	*Ronan Noone*	190
Thoughts at the End of a Sunny Day	*Regina Hennelly*	193
The Most Embarrassing Moment of My Life	*Callum Spence*	195
The Guinness Man	*Garret Pearse*	199
The Last Visit	*Martin Fitzgerald*	201
The Biscuit Tin	*Des Cox*	204
Pink Chiffon	*Sheila Donohue*	208
A Sports Car and a Boyfriend	*Fiona Cullinan*	210
December's Work	*Noeleen Kavanagh*	213
Cut Up when Cold	*Liz Macguire*	215
An Irish Waking	*Caren Kennedy*	217
My Mother Wears a Car on the Third Finger of Her Left Hand	*Jane Travers*	219
The Human Spirit Is Alive and Well in Haiti	*Mary Donohoe*	221
Index of Authors		223

Foreword by Matt Cooper,
Presenter of *The Last Word*, Today FM

We all have our stories. Some good, some bad. Some that we will tell to a small number of people, maybe just one person – others we might like to broadcast to as many as will listen. Some we will never reveal to anyone for reasons we may never wish to disclose. Some stories are about things we wish hadn't happened or had worked out differently or of which we are very proud. Or that just made us laugh or cry and we want to share. Some stories are interesting, even riveting, to us but not to anyone else. Some we think are of no significance but have something in them from which others can draw plenty.

This is a book of such stories. They are true stories. Perhaps some are embellished – and I'm not pointing you in any particular direction – but in any case there's no harm in that if they strike a chord or engage and entertain you more than they might otherwise have done. As long, of course, as they do no deliberate harm to those who may be identified by the text. Some may have been self-edited so as not to cause hurt or embarrassment to the subjects or just to make them better. There's no harm in that either.

The stories in this book will appeal to a variety of people. Different stories will do different things for different people. But sometimes a book of short stories like this is like a good restaurant menu. Imagine you are sitting down to a nice meal and that you have been presented with the menu. There may be many things on the list from which you choose and among those there are some you think you are going to like or that you are sure you won't. But in a good restaurant if you get your starter, your main course and your dessert, with something good to drink as well, you may be very satisfied indeed, irrespective of what else is offered to you. You may also find that the chance you take in trying something about which you are doubtful turns out to be inspired or inspiring.

In any case these are stories that were offered by their writers and published to support an excellent cause: disaster relief in Haiti.

There are many stories to be told about Haiti. Many of them are harrowing and some are uplifting. Those of us who have never visited the country have been hearing them them since the day of that awful, devastating earthquake early in 2010, which visited destruction and death upon one of the very poorest countries in the world. There are stories of despair and of courage, of death and of life.

There are stories too of the Irish who have gone there, although this is not a book about them. That is for another day.

This is a book of Irish stories, about the ordinariness and extraordinariness of our lives here in Ireland that makes us what we are and makes us the people willing to help the less fortunate abroad. It is a book that serves the dual purpose of providing enjoyment to ourselves and help to others.

Providence

Michael Owens, Bray, County Wicklow

Old Man Levine never spoke to me except to say, 'Hello, hello, hello,' and I knew nothing about him or what country he came from. Someone once told me he came from Europe to escape anti-Semitism and the Nazis and the Irish government gave him refuge. I was too young to understand any of this. To me he was just a Dublin Jew who taught me a mystery: the universe provides and only the very young and the very old truly believe it. Those in between are short on trust.

He had a routine. In the afternoon he would close his front door and stand on the footpath. In soft hat and overcoat, summer and winter, he would wait until he was sure he was seen. Then he would shuffle, hands in his pockets, down the street. He never looked to the right or to the left. All the kids would follow saying, 'Hello, hello'. He would reply, 'Hello, hello, hello,' and pennies from heaven would fall to the ground. It was a good trick and I never understood how he did it. The pennies would appear from nowhere like manna on the desert floor. There was a never-ending supply and always a penny for everyone, which we spent on sweets at McGrath's.

I always wondered how he knew how many kids would be on the street on any given day. Now I think he just believed he'd have enough for the need. This was the message he imparted on those afternoons: the universe provides.

I found this to be true. When I was very young my days were full. I didn't have to fill them up. The fullness was already there.

Days came complete. I didn't need to pray, 'Give me this day my daily bread.' Needs were met in the day's play and I never stopped to think I could want for more. The bread of heaven came to me fresh every morning. Life was full of surprises. Every day I asked, 'What is it?' Every day was a wonder. Every day there was something new. I ate manna from heaven and was satisfied. Providence smiled upon me, although I didn't know what it was at the time. I just knew I was in safe hands, that life provided and the world was mine. I never needed. The old Jew gave me that knowledge, an old man who had the look of the Ancients about him and a twinkle in his eyes.

When the Jews saw manna on the desert floor they asked, 'What is it?' Manna means, 'What is it?' Moses said, 'It is the bread the Lord has given you to eat.' Manna is what we find along the way. The manna I found on any given day was life's provision for survival. The Jews lived on manna until they arrived at the border of Canaan and I suppose Old Man Levine did too in Dublin long ago.

I'm a long way from Warren Street now and I'm not very young and I'm not very old. I'm in-between and short on trust. My body aches and my head hurts and I complain too much. Every day seems the same. There's nothing new in my life and I live by daily routine. Still I rise every morning hoping to be surprised, hoping I might ask again, 'What is it?'

But then I think how foolish I am. I've had a sweet life that any wandering Jew would have envied. I am content. I have my routine like Old Man Levine. I don't need to ask, 'What is it.' I know.

A Tribute to the Large Family

Mary Lynch, Castlerea, County Roscommon

Coming from a large family has to be one of the best experiences for any soul, if you are lucky enough, like me, to come from this kind of family: even if you don't meet one another or even speak to one another for long periods of time, you know you can pick up again as if you were finishing yesterday's conversation.

Growing up, I never thought it was unusual to be part of a large family (because it wasn't) until, at the age of nineteen I made my escape to West Germany to get away from it all – and them all, if the truth be known. For six glorious months I had no family and no way of contacting them, as in 1979 there were no mobiles, no internet, no Facebook, no Skype, not even a phone – just the post that took weeks.

There in Germany I was not only free of a war but of any one stealing my jeans off the line, including my brother, who left for Dublin every Monday morning with everything he could take off the line and that included all the jeans. (At that time, five of us wore Size 28 Wranglers, the only brand available or affordable.)

In Germany I was free. I did have to share a room with a snooty German girl but she was not my sister and I could pretend I did not understand her, which I did regularly.

The Germans would ask me questions to improve their English, like how many children were in my family?

When I answered that I had seven brothers and four sisters everyone came to ask the same question as they did not believe it was possible, The second question was invariably, 'How many times was your father married?'

My God, I thought at the beginning, will I tell them that we were a regular, good Irish Catholic family that had no choice in any of this or even say that there were seventeen in the neighbour's family.

It was only after I had learnt a few German words that I realised that *eins* was one and *zwei* was two and their families never got any bigger than that. This was when they were being given a year off work for maternity leave – and that was just for the men.

They would sit in amazement and then ask me what size house we lived in. Did we have a cook? A cleaner?' Like their mothers had, to take care of the 1.5 children.

'How does your mother cope?' was the next question, to which I answered with amusement, 'As she always did, one day at a time.'

I was beginning to feel like a freak until one night at a party someone asked, after a few drinks, 'What is it really like, I mean *really* like?'

And after a few drinks, I answered, 'It's like having eleven best friends who cannot refuse you anything if you really push it as you share the same blood.

'You always had lots of boys coming to the house to pick up or drop off one of your seven brothers and even if you were fussy, there was always a good chance of meeting someone of the opposite sex without ever having to leave home.

'There was always someone who knew someone who could help you out with whatever it was you wanted, if you could convince them to help you.

'No matter what happened to you they would always be there for you, even if only to tell you you were a bollocks and should have known better.

'They always had a solution to your problems, even when you did not even know you had a problem, as they were looking out for you.'

When I returned home they did not seem such a bad bunch and then when I moved to New York City in 1980 during a recession in Ireland, a lot of them followed me. The States were booming and I spent the next six years getting them jobs, apartments and furniture until I moved home in 1986 (to a recession) and they continued to do the same for the others that followed. Then guess what? They all eventually followed me home again (when the recession was over).

Thirty years after that first move away from them, nothing has changed, apart from our ages and another recession.

I still get clothes handed down to me even though the clothes belong to my niece, with expensive taste, I'm glad to say, not a big brown box from America.

When we all congregate for an occasion, the energy there would lift the room.

You have a female elder to whom you could chat endlessly about how you were coping after your separation, especially with teenagers, and she would listen patiently, then telling you her problems.

You have big men to threaten any other males if they push themselves on you. You might not dream of asking for help but in your head it was a option, saved for the last straw. The option had to be used only once in fifty years, when I had nearly reached that age, and it worked like a dream and I was so proud I asked and he was so proud he could help.

You know, however smart or well dressed the sisters look, that you can remember them as skinny, snotty-nosed children, especially the younger ones who now have small children, making us older girls feel like grannies and loving it as we play with the children, then leave them back. Our own by this time are all grown up (or imagine they are).

We can spend endless hours taking about how tough we were brought up and all we learnt so that we could take with a pinch of salt our so-called stressful lives when we look back on what stress really was, being brought up in a war.

And finally it's a great thing to know that whatever happens in your life, eleven other people out there love you unconditionally.

Thirty years later we in Ireland have come to resemble Germany of the late 1970s with our 1.5 children.

Now when people ask how many are in my family, I can still say twelve. They still ask me what it was like.

I answer just as I have always have done, and when they continue, 'And how did your parents cope?' I say, one day at a time, but now they live alone, taking care of each other and still keeping an eye on us all, in their eighty-second and ninety-second year.

The Waterford Connection

Pat Hanrahan, County Tipperary (now living in New York)

In *Triggering Town* the author, Richard Hugo, refers to his disappointment when he and his wife made a return visit to Italy in 1963. He remembered it during World War II as 'brown and grey and lifeless'. He had 'fallen in love with a sad land' and that was what he expected to find. Now he found it 'filled with sparkling fountains and shiny little cars that honked and darted through well-kept streets'.

The Ireland I left in 1964 resembled the Italy that he describes so vividly and some years later, when I became involved in the marketing side of selling Ireland, I found it was the youthful, vibrant and shiny Ireland like Italy in 1963 that was being sold. This came home to me again and again when Aer Lingus and/or the Irish Tourist Board received letters from disappointed customers. One I recall vividly came from a woman who had been convinced from the advertising that the new Ireland was a long way from the Ireland she remembered but hadn't visited in years.

'To whom it may concern:

'And not for a minute do I think you people are concerned, as you already have my money. I have just returned from a most disappointing trip to Ireland, where I found that parts of the country are still in the dark ages. I left Ireland forty years ago because I had no choice and had been looking forward to my first trip back, now that my children are done for. My travel agent Mr Grimes, I'm sure you know him, assured me that Ireland was very up to date. Modern was the word he used and it certainly looks like that from the pictures and posters.

'It may well be, but not if you're trying to get by train from Kilkenny to Limerick. As the crow flies, the towns are about fifty miles apart, but in this day and age there is still no direct train service. I ask you, how can this be between two of the largest and busiest towns in the country? You people can't even imagine the hassle of changing trains in Waterford, as I'm sure you've never had to do it.

'The train from Kilkenny took its time leaving the station. Well, it was supposed to leave at eleven o'clock but at precisely that time (I checked my watch) I spotted the train-driver stepping down from his cab and heading for the men's room. I ask you: how can that be tolerated? If it were I, or one of the other passengers, we would surely have been left behind. The train then ambled into Waterford nicely late and I just knew I had missed my connection.

'I spotted a young man in a uniform and asked him about the connecting train to Limerick. He was very quick to tell me there was no such train. I was equally quick to show him my ticket and the timetable. He then told me in a surly manner that they were working on the track and I'd have to go to Limerick by bus. When I asked him where it left from he just laughed and said it was gone already. My train was late and the bus just left. I ask you: is this any way to run a railroad?

'When I asked him who was in charge he nodded towards the station master's office and went off about his business. What a saint that man proved to be. He apologised for my inconvenience, made a quick phone call to the bus driver, told him to pull over and drove me out the road after the bus.

'Now, Aer Lingus and the Irish Tourist Board, what do you make of that? Is that any way to treat visitors to holy Ireland? What are you going to do about it is my question? The bus and train drivers should be fired and that young pup at Waterford station needs to have manners put on him. If it weren't for the station master, God bless him, I'd be still trying to find my way to Limerick.

'I look forward to hearing from you with an explanation and a refund.'

Unfortunately this letter did the rounds in our little circle and was seen as hilarious. Eventually, a junior clerk at the Tourist Board drafted a response but it was a form letter with a generic apology. 'Putting manners' on someone became a catchphrase and the source of much hilarity. Mr Hugo was right when he said, 'It helps when you don't have any feelings to hide,' with reference to senior management in industry.

Our Lady of Dublin

Nuala Ní Chonchúir, Ballinasloe, County Galway

Whenever I go abroad I like to visit churches in order to feed my fascination for religious iconography. In particular, I am very taken by statues of the Virgin Mary. Something about her melancholy eyes and slender form as she cradles her baby reaches me and makes me want to linger and stare.

In Brussels a few years ago I hauled myself off the main drag in search of the church of Saint Catherine. I knew it was home to a statue of the Holy Mother and Child called the Black Madonna. The church stood on a quiet market square and inside we found the carved stone statuette. She was partitioned behind glass in the central nave, presumably to save her from her from a fate like the previous one. In 14th century Belgium this Black Madonna was tossed into the River Seine by Protestants but somehow landed on a clod of peat and was rescued and given a secure home in Saint Catherine's.

We have our own Black Madonna in Ireland, a fact that was brought to my attention by my father. Her domain is the Carmelite Church on Dublin's Whitefriar Street and she is known as Our Lady of Dublin. This magnificent statue of the Virgin and Child, reputedly carved from German oak, dates from the time of the Reformation. The wooden body is stained a deep, dark brown as rich colours weren't allowed in churches in Reformation times.

Our Lady of Dublin is placed high in a shrine and her dark body is highlighted by the jewelled crown on her head and the white marble and golden mosaic that surround her. Our Lady herself appears subdued but the child Jesus, who is tucked into the folds of her robe, seems to be leaping in her arms.

Like Belgium's Black Madonna, Our Lady of Dublin has an interesting past. Her original home was St Mary's Abbey on the north side of the Liffey. During the 16th century, when monasteries were destroyed and their treasures stolen or ruined, Mary's Abbey was used as a stable. The statue of Our Lady of Dublin was taken from the abbey and the length of her wooden back was hollowed out. She was placed face down in an inn yard and put to use as a trough for feeding pigs. In this way she was almost certainly saved from being destroyed.

In the mid 1800s the wooden statue with its hollowed back was discovered in a pawnshop on Capel Street by Father John Spratt, the prior of Whitefriar Street, the same man, incidentally, who brought the remains of Saint Valentine to Dublin. Father Spratt transported the unusual statue across the Liffey to his church and gave Our Lady a safe home there.

A couple of years ago, when I knew my partner was going to pop the question, I warned him to 'pick somewhere good'. In the event, we went to Dublin. On a dark December night, just before Christmas, he brought me in a taxi from our posh hotel to Whitefriar Street and, there, under the watchful eyes of Our Lady of Dublin and Saint Valentine, we got engaged. I couldn't have asked for a more thoughtful spot to seal our love.

When I revisited the shrine recently and gazed at the virgin statue in the lively atmosphere of the church, I couldn't help thinking that we have a habit in Ireland of underselling the riches we possess. After all, treasures are treasures no matter how large or how small they are. We may not have a Notre Dame or a Canterbury, but we are lucky enough to have Whitefriar Street church and Our Lady of Dublin.

Hurry Home

Linda Gillett, Shankill, County Dublin

The last leg of the long journey home was a blur and it was only then, in the car, that he let his guard down. His view through the windscreen was obscured by tears, his heart constricted by fear. His only company was the cat, mewing sorrowfully in the box on the passenger seat. She had told him the blanket would quieten the cat, that darkness would allay its fear. The blanket wasn't working. What did she know about anything, he thought. She didn't even have the sense to ask for help until it was almost too late. He wished someone would throw a blanket around him, smother his terrible pain and comfort him.

He had left her in the hospital, to go home and begin restoring some structure to their lives, blown to pieces firstly by pneumonia and now by organ failure. The first few hours of the New Year had thrown them into a medical maelstrom. After three days in a foreign hospital and an air ambulance home, she was settled into her fourth-floor high-dependency unit overlooking the grey expanse of Dublin Bay, enduring the same round of tests and questions, which he had to answer for her.

Now it was safe for him to leave her and go home, collect the cat and unpack the car. Unpacking wouldn't take long. There was only one bag, containing the essentials for emergency travel: passports, medical notes, insurance documents, toiletries, medicine, wallets, unused flight tickets, tissues, blanket, underwear. The jet home had room for only six people – two pilots, two medics, patient and husband – and no luggage. DHL would ship their cases later. It would make for a good story some time, he thought. For a second he allowed himself to imagine laughing about their holiday calamity with the lads over a pint. Then he checked himself. Only if she – they – came through this.

He was back so soon after leaving that he half-expected to meet himself in the hall. To go back in time was all he wanted to do – then maybe they could have been able to avoid all this. What would he have said to himself if he had? 'Don't go. Can't you tell she's dying? She doesn't see it but you can.' The house was cold and dark. The floor tiles in the hall reflected January's chill and it seeped into his bones. Coming home to an empty house was unusual to him. She would always be home first and have some concoction bubbling away on the hob and the curtains closing out the staring night. Now, there was no welcome home hug and loneliness slapped him in the face.

The cat's complaints brought him back to his senses. Once released, the creature readjusted to its familiar surroundings in a matter of minutes. It sniffed the cat food he teased out of the pouch and looked at him. Could it see his broken heart, he wondered? Could it sense something was wrong?

In preparation for their intended three-week holiday in Florida, the fridge had been cleared of all food. It was too late for a takeaway now. He could handle the hunger for a few more hours. It was more important to make phone calls anyway. This had been his main role in all the panic of the past few days and he grasped at it: it was his way of taking control, playing a part. It was his skill in negotiation that won out in the phone debate with the medical insurance company. Now he strategically called friends who would help to spread the word, saving him hours of repeating the heart-breaking story; he talked into the night to his shocked relatives and found comfort in their promises of prayer. He knew Galway would be alight with candles tonight. But all these parts didn't add up to the sum of his missing wife.

The day had run away from him, his time taken up with family conferences, phone calls and doctor briefings. He had absorbed all that the specialists told him about her chances and had relayed the news sensitively to her fragile family, watching how they crumbled from its impact. He had spent the rest of his time with her, feeling the walls of the small ward close in and the smells of disinfectant and mashed potato turn his stomach.

He was grateful now for the cat's bad habit of sleeping on the bed. It protested grumpily as he climbed in between the cold white sheets to share its small circle of heat, then resettled under his arm. His head spun as his brain processed all the day's events, making no concession to jet lag or emotional fatigue. Then the whine of silence in his ears paved the way to a sleep of days, of years, that was needed to soak up his weariness and provide him with the strength to help her to carry on. He felt himself drift on a calm sea of wishes and hopes. A most delicious sleep awaited, and he welcomed a complete, if temporary, resignation of all that he could do.

He heard a gentle voice reassuring him that everything was going to be OK and the wait was over. But it wasn't his wife. And he was not dreaming. He found himself slowly replacing the phone receiver, sitting upright in bed, lights exploding in his head and heart. A donor organ had been found.

Linda's husband, Noel Marytn, writes: 'Linda passed away on 23 June 2010 after a truly heroic battle with cancer. She was thirty-six years of age. Some weeks before she died she told me that she had written a story about the build-up to her liver transplant told from my perspective, and that she had submitted the story to the Concern anthology. After Linda died I discovered the story and I mentioned it in my eulogy at her funeral Mass.'

Firsts

Jody Collins, Dublin (originally from Connecticut, USA)

I was six when my father, mother, sister, myself and the dog got on a plane and moved to Haiti. My father was going to spend a year of his surgical residency working in the Hospital Albert Schweitzer in the Artibonite Valley and I began my education. It was my first time on a plane. My father told me to watch for the toilet paper flying by the window when someone went in to use the toilet. It was my first time living under a tin roof that sounded as if it was under gunfire attack when the pregnant humidity of the day finally gave way to grey downpours of rain. It was my first time watching peanuts being roasted and smashed for thick, handmade peanut butter with oil that floated to the top. It was my first sight of hunger, first experience of funeral marches with children's caskets, the first feel of the beat of ritual drums in the hills and the first acceptance of the stories of the zombies that walked after dark that would keep me listening long into the night-time when the world went silent.

My parents bought all the remembrances they could carry back – wooden bowls, woven baskets, carved statues and paintings – painting of people with thin faces and huge staring eyes that sat disproportionate and haunting. Primitive faces with relentless eyes trying to make sense of the chaos of a place of tragedy and magic.

I was twenty-six when I moved to Ireland to continue my education. I imagined the toilet paper floating by my window as I always do when we are cruising at 30, 000 feet over the Atlantic.

It was my first time alone so far away from home. It was the first time of many that I would arrive in a place that I had only heard of, with two bags and a list of phone numbers. It was the first time I stayed in hotels alone until I found a place with a window that was visited in the mornings by the first pair of magpies I had ever seen…one for sorrow, two for joy. Ireland. It was my first creamy bitter sip of stout; my first heartbeat beating in time with a bodhrán. It was my first understanding of famine and how it leaves scars on a people and how the horrors of a tragedy are hushed and muted until its silent imprint makes a vacuum in what was the warmth of a hearth and the melody of a song. It was my first walk through an abandoned western village that overlooked the sea and whispered the stories of its dead and exiled.

And it was in my first dimly-lit walk past the *Book of Kells* I saw again those relentlessly staring eyes, eyes the size of saucers, staring from the words of the gospel. Primitive faces with relentless eyes trying to make sense of the chaos of a place of tragedy and magic.

A Pint and a Haircut

James Smith, Cavan

After fifty years in the pub business my father recently retired. In those fifty years he put together a collection of stories that you wouldn't believe and that are a reflection of Irish life from 1959 to 2009.

My father was the type of publican who valued every one of his customers and the craic that each one brought to the pub. He would rather lose money on drinks than lose a customer. As long as customers weren't insulting someone, fighting or generally being a nuisance they were always welcomed.

It was one of these customers who in the 1970s realised that farmers bringing milk to the local creamery didn't have time for a drink *and* a haircut and decided to set up a barber's shop in the toilets of the pub. He would come in every Friday, have a few whiskeys and a couple of pints of Guinness and then take one of the bar stools into the toilets. The farmers would wait patiently at the bar for their haircut.

For the first couple of weeks my father didn't realise what was going on. When he finally caught on to what was happening, he decided that as long as the 'barber' wasn't too drunk while cutting the hair and didn't clip the top of someone's ear off, why not let it go.

This went on for about six months and it became such a part of the life of the pub that no one thought it was strange. That is until an off-duty member of the Garda Special Branch from Adare felt nature calling. He went into the toilet and encountered a slightly inebriated barber cutting the hair of an even more inebriated customer. The three men nodded at one another and went about their business.

After that day the Garda became a regular of the pub until the day my father closed the doors for good. He reckoned that in all the pubs in Ireland that he had visited, he had never encountered a sight like this. This was a pub where virtually anything could happen and he wanted to be there if it did.

Silas

Paul Reidy, Dublin (former Concern volunteer)

He turned to look squarely at me. For a brief moment I thought from the look in his eyes that he was challenging my authority and a wave of embarrassment passed over me. I showed him nothing, though – I had long since learned how to disguise such emotions from Silas. Nonetheless I felt ashamed at the carelessness and throwaway nature of my remark when he was so confused and frightened that day, as they all were.

'And why do you think we're leaving, Mister Paul? Do you think we want to cross that border, to be killed – or even worse imprisoned? Where have you been this last while?'

'I'm sorry, Silas,' I replied. 'I was just thinking aloud.'

I couldn't be sure but it looked like he shook his head at me. This was so unlike the Silas I had grown to know so well that I hoped he didn't think too poorly of me after all this time. Not now. I wanted so desperately for us to part on a level of mutual respect, professionally if not personally.

He took his usual seat behind his desk in our camp HQ and stared at me in silence for some time, not unkindly but uncomfortably. His face was drawn, lined and stressed. He was clearly exhausted. 'Sit down, Mister Paul, please!' he said at last. 'I have a parting gift for you.'

Outside, the long day was coming to an end. The half-light crept quickly over Ngara. Fifteen minutes of twilight was all the time we had left. It was Christmas week and somewhere in the distance were groups of people chatting loudly, perhaps downing the last of their banana beer in a futile effort to dull their senses. And then that solo voice rose above the din, a female one singing 'Usiku Kimya' – 'Silent Night'. It was at once the most beautiful and saddest sound I had ever heard.

'We've worked together for how long now, Mister Paul?'

'Three months. Well, closer to four.'

'Ah, yes,' he said. 'Four months. Four good months. We worked well together, you and I. We had some good times, yes?'

'Sure, Silas. Yes.'

'And you know that tomorrow I am going to die.'

'Going to die, Silas?' I said in outrage. 'That's ridiculous! Stop thinking that way. You're not going to die. Just explain to them that you're innocent; that you had nothing to do with any of it. I'll write you a reference letter, for God's sake. I'll tell them.'

My voice had begun to rise and my cheeks were hot. But as I spoke Silas just sat quietly, a sad smile upon his lips. He clearly knew something I did not.

He opened the bottom drawer of his desk and removed a sealed envelope with my name written neatly upon it. 'Open it when I'm gone,' he said. 'Promise me to wait until then.'

'You'll be fine, Silas. Things will work out, you'll see.'

'Promise me!' he urged.

'OK, I promise,' I said. 'I promise.'

We shook hands as we had done that first day when he stood at the foot of the steps of the ten-seater plane that had brought me from Mwanza to a machete-cleared strip of runway on the Tanzania-Rwanda border. 'Mr Paul, I presume,' he said. 'I'm Silas, camp manager of Lumasi Refugee Camp. I am here to help.'

I was soon to realise that he was a man of his word.

We waited for three days in the safety of our expatriate compound, nine kilometres from the Rwandan border, as the Tanzanian army moved into Lumasi. We had expected to hear much shooting in the distance over our Christmas turkey dinner which had been flown in from Dublin to make us all feel a little less homesick. With half a million or so reluctant refugees on the move again, the silence was eerie.

By St Stephen's Day, the job was successfully completed. I remember that it was a particularly beautiful morning, the sun still low enough in the sky to throw shadows of the few remaining trees on the red clay. There were twenty or so of us, volunteers from the remaining organisations, a search party, standing in a line to sweep the camp, sector by sector, checking every individual mud hut to see if any vulnerable people had been left behind in the furore of the sudden exodus. Who needed the old and infirm to slow them down under such circumstances? No one knew what lay across the border.

Some of my expatriate colleagues that day had reported standing at the roadside on Christmas Eve, watching people move down the surrounding hills like colonies of ants. It was true that there was hardly a sound to be heard but the heavy tramping of feet. They held sacks of their belongings above their heads, while smiling children skipped and waved to their *munzugu* (white man) spectators. As they spoke, I could think of little else but Silas and his young family, praying they had made it home alive.

We began to scour the huts in groups along designated routes, one by one. It had not occurred to me before how little I truly knew of this camp that I had managed for so long. It looked different. Some of the huts were hidden away behind bigger ones. Some were so large they had a number of rooms and an internal pit-latrine or two. In the market square – a clearing close to one of the food distribution centres – were barber's and tailor's shops, restaurants and bars. It was a small functioning city like any other, all abandoned in a matter of days. It painted a lonely picture. Then, near Buffalo Crossing – an intersection that saw a poor, confused buffalo approach one day, some time before my arrival, unprepared for the hungry excited chase that ensued and his capture and clubbing to death – I found Silas's hut. I had been there only once before but I recognised it instantly. It was what I had come to find.

I entered, bending so as not to strike my head off the low frame. At first it seemed like any other hut – humid, bare but for some straw mats with a leftover tin cup or two. But when my eyes adjusted to the light, I noticed that there in the corner of the room were flimsy Christmas decorations made from bits of discarded cardboard and paper from the boxes and tins that we had so often distributed to the camp population. He had been taking them home with him habitually after work, something I had noticed but never bothered to question him about. Now, as I stood in the house that he had occupied for two and a half years, a house where his wife had given birth to twins, I saw him working late at night in the dark, in the painful build-up to Christmas, to bring some sense of normality, some sense of hope perhaps, to the madness of his situation.

I remembered the promise I had made him and, removing the envelope from my pocket, I tore it open there and then. It was a photograph, taken shortly after my arrival to Lumasi, of Silas and me, lifting a sack of maize on to the back of a truck. We were laughing for some reason – I can't recall why. On the back he had written the following message:

To my very good friend, Mister Paul –
Joyeux Noël and a Merry Christmas.
May God bless you and your family always.
Silas,
Ngara 1996

I read it a number of times and cried unashamedly. Never in my life had I felt so far away from home.

THE CHANTYPOE CHAMPION

Jack O'Donnell, Scotland

God did not make the same promise to Charlie Porter that He made to Abraham: that his descendents would be like grains of sands on the beach. There were no blaring trumpets or angels calling, just snotty noses and the promise of a council house in Linnvale. But Josie had two gentle hands for mothering and a soft lilting voice that could woo any child back from the abyss. Charlie's voice was of a rougher grain, sandpaper on open ears. It came from the depths of rural Ireland and flung out enough 'rrrrrrs' to start a tractor and when that didn't work, moved up another gear and 'RRRRed' enough to make me fidget and float away, to collect bumblebees in a jar, because I only spoke the idiot English.

Later, when I'd mastered the language of the Woodbine Full Strength, the half of whisky and the half of beer, Charlie was working for a fellow Irishman. Only Spratt, the gaffer, could have seen that a triangle of land between the Ging-Gang-Gooley Scout Hall, with a railway at its back and a garage on the other side, full of ground elder and bindweed, was good for nothing – but making money. Spratt planted a two-bob caravan and four men from Letterkenny bloomed into being. Some men might have called him an entrepreneur, for if there were contracts to be won and holes to be dug in the road, there was no need for expensive equipment; all he needed was Letterkenny men to fill them. And if God in his foresight didn't give them enough light, Spratt made sure the tick of the diesel generator would eke out enough fumes to fill a light bulb.

Charlie got on his bike and migrated north out of Linnvale and found himself in the same hole as the Letterkenny men. But he soon showed them a clean pair of heels, for although he was small, he skipped and danced through any kind of navvy work he tackled, like Celtic's great Jimmy Johnstone on the wing.

Later, when I met Charlie at a funeral of his old comrade, he had one hand holding the cuff of his black jacket and his left foot was trailing behind him, marking his shiny shoes. He still talked out of the side of his mouth, like a penny-whistle gangster, but complained that he'd had a stroke; life had slowed him down and it had taken him two days to paint the whole house.

Sadly, he said, he couldn't smoke Woodbine any more and had to settle for some Silk Cut spectre of a cigarette with a tip. After a few jars we always returned to the subject of Spratt and the glory days. Charlie would always be in the front of the wagon. The Goat would be in the back, for as Charlie said, 'the Goat might have been the gaffer, but even if you shat in both his Wellington boots he couldn't have smelt any worse. You couldn't have such a man sitting beside you. That would be indecent.'

Charlie, Charlie, always at the top of his game.

Speech! Speech!

Ian O'Malley, Carlow

The cry goes up. The call for words. This need to verbalise the communal experience. Yep, Irish people love speeches.

I was sitting in the passenger seat of Andrew's green van. We were turning right over Graiguecullen Bridge when he asked me to be best man at his wedding. He was nervous about asking me. For reasons explained below.

Survey by Philadelphia State University, Department of Humanities, 2007: 'People's Top Ten Greatest Fears':

Number 2: 'Speaking in Public'.

The average Irish person doesn't necessarily love standing in front of a large group of people and making a speech themselves. But the average Irish person does seem to have an inexplicable compulsion to make other people make speeches. Think of any event. The birthday party, the farewell dinner, the table quiz to raise money for the local camogie team…At some point the crowd will bay at the poor victim who happens to be the centre of attention for the night, 'Speech! Speech!' Mumble a few embarrassed words or grab the moment and let it all out there. Either way, you have to say something; they won't let you escape.

While living in Italy, I noticed a different phenomenon. I was at a joint birthday party for two Italian friends; I was the only non-Italian present. The moment came for the big presentation of gifts and subconsciously I was expecting to hear it: "Speech! Speech!', the familiar refrain. 'Nudi! Nudi!' they all shouted instead. No call for speeches at all. Just, 'Nude! Nude! Get your clothes off!' Has its merits.

I was at a Spanish wedding. The meal went on for hours, five courses. The drink flowed. There were flamenco dancers, cigars brought around for all the men, countless noisy toasts to the happy couple, a Spanish guitar serenade, more food, music till 6am. No speeches.

Speeches are central to an Irish wedding. You know what the average outlay on a wedding was at the height of the Celtic Tiger? €30,000. Yes, €30,000. Yes, the average. Ice-sculpted swans and bows on chairs, chocolate fountains and bouquets of flowers coming out your arse, whatever it took to make the most important day of your life a*bsolutely perfect*. (Be honest with yourself, how many of those a*bsolutely perfect* weddings you attended did you find *incredibly tedious*?)

Regardless of the expense, one thing Irish people invariably comment on after a wedding is the speeches. These stick in people's memories, especially the bad ones. Remember the speeches that went on for far, far too long? Remember the 'ems' and 'ahs' and the 'Where was I?' The fumbling with notes. The jokes that fell flat. The throwaway comment that left some female relative in tears.

A speech I particularly enjoyed was one by the father of the groom at a wedding I attended. He had (and this resulted in a certain amount of controversy) missed his son's marriage ceremony because he was still drunk from the night before. His speech consisted of just three words: 'Let's get pissed.'

Andrew had been my best friend since we were teenagers. He was nervous asking me to be his best man because he wasn't sure what my answer would be. I might have said no. We weren't friends any more. It wasn't that had we drifted apart or anything. No, we'd fallen out badly and suddenly and our friendship had never recovered.

The best man's speech. The most anticipated one of all. You

know the format: the best man drags up every old story to humiliate the groom. I'd never really understood why that is so. But now? Now, I had the chance and the means, the vehicle, to express all the hurt and resentment I'd felt for so long towards Andrew. On this day of all days, in front of everybody. And he'd given me this chance himself. Vengeance…

Nah. Obviously not. Andrew asking me to be his best man was all the gesture of reconciliation that was needed. I embraced it.

I had a look at some books on best man's speeches. All crap. I thought about previous speeches I'd heard, thought of all the clichés and lazy jokes I wanted to avoid. I wanted to do this right. Make people laugh. Get the right mix of jokes and being genuine. Andrew deserved for me to come up with something original, worthy of him, of the gesture he'd made, worthy of the glorious, transcendent friendship we'd once had and hoped to have again.

So, on a sunny day in September, I stood up nervously in front of everybody at Andrew's wedding: his new wife, parents, his brother, his sister, all his friends. No pressure, I told myself. The expectant faces were all looking at me, waiting for me. People will remember this for years to come only if you mess it up, I told myself. Someone said to me beforehand they'd be watching to see if my hands were shaking. They definitely were shaking. Andrew said to me with that smile of his, 'Don't hold back, lad. Let me have it.'

I began. 'Being Andrew's best man and thinking what advice I can offer to him for his future married life is kind of strange because when we were young lads he was always the one giving me advice on love and girls. And on the basis of that advice, I didn't have my first proper girlfriend until I was twenty-five. So cheers for that, lad…'

All the jokes worked. I didn't insult anyone, didn't go on

too long. I expressed sincerely-felt sentiments without being mawkish or clunky. Afterwards, one uncle of the bride gave me a score of ninety-seven out of a hundred for the best speech he'd heard in ages. Andrew gave me a big hug. So did his wife. It felt so good. Relief. And a wave of exhaustion. Much later on, one of the pretty bridesmaids, who thought my speech was 'hilarious', let me walk her back to her hotel-room door and gave me a kiss goodnight on the cheek. Yippee! I was easily pleased.

Making that speech as Andrew's best man was the thing that did most to heal the estrangement from each other we'd experienced for so long. Putting our friendship into words made us both realise how much it meant. How much we'd missed each other and still liked each other… if that all doesn't sound too trite.

The end.

No, not really.

Nine months later, there was a call for another speech.

Survey by Philadelphia State University, Department of Humanities, 2007: 'People's Top Ten Greatest Fears':

Number 1: 'Fear of Death'.

Four o'clock in the morning, the room silent. Andrew's father was huddled in an armchair opposite me. His eyes were scrunched closed and there was a cup of cold tea in his trembling hands. He asked me if I'd make a speech about Andrew again.

Ten hours before, Andrew had worked and chatted. He was still a bit hungover from a party the night before. He called his wife to say he was on his way home. Then, he just died. Heart stopped. Fell to the ground. Mid-sentence.

On a pissy, rainy day in June, I stood up in front of everybody to speak at Andrew's funeral. His wife, his brother, his sister, his mother and father. Everybody. The same faces from nine months before. Nobody said to me they'd be watching to see if my hands were shaking. My whole body was shaking and grief-stricken and determined. My knees were buckling inside my stupid black suit.

How do you put this into words? No books to guide you now. Jokes? Genuine? Does it matter?

It mattered to me.

I felt the crushing weight of this responsibility as I'd never felt anything n my life. Being asked to deliver this speech gave me a sense of honour that will never leave me – ever.

Put words on your friend's life. Open your mouth. Go on. Speak. They're looking at you, waiting for you. The expectant faces. Pleading for you to say something. You're good at this. You know you are. Go on. No one else has the strength to do this now. This one little thing you're good at. Make a speech. Go on. Get it right.

'Don't hold back, lad. Let me have it,' Andrew would have said to me with that smile of his. 'You're my best friend. I'm glad it's you doing this.'

I began, 'I first met Andrew when I was thirteen years old...'

The Prisoner's Dilemma

John Butler, Dublin

It is annoying how more often than not my homeward tube terminates a single stop before my destination and I have to wait for the next train to take me one stop further, a distance that could nearly (but not quite) be walked with ease. There is a choice of course, but it's the prisoner's dilemma – wait at Picadilly for the right train to take you home, or take the train fast approaching, get off closer to home and wait there. Usually I take whichever train comes first. I would rather do my waiting closer to home. There, I can argue with myself about whether I should be walking the rest of the way home instead of waiting around and this dialogue occupies me on the platform until the right train arrives.

That's where my mind was on a dark Wednesday night when out of the corner of my eye I saw a homeless man approaching the person furthest away from me, examining them in silence and then moving along, slowly. He was not speaking to anyone, merely walking up to them deliberately, sizing them up, arriving at some conclusion about them based on their appearance, then shuffling along. He was maybe fifty, clean-shaven but with matted hair and a Lord Anthony anorak with a fluffy collar.

About eight of us were waiting, equidistant from one another, facing the tracks. We weren't talking or searching for eye contact, because these are the rules of train-waiting. And fascinatingly, this man was breaking those rules, staring right at an individual from a matter of feet away, then deciding something and moving on to the next passenger. What was he was looking for? Was it the set of a jaw, the colour of hair, or the type of clothes? I was still listening to music when he came near me but I had turned it down to hear if he was saying anything to the person next to me. He said nothing to them, then came towards me and stopped right in front of me, a few feet away. My turn. I felt a twinge of nerves. Along the platform I could see one or two passengers glancing down to see what he made of me.

The wind whipped along the platform as the man looked into my eyes and finally, I looked into his. For some reason, I wanted it to go well. Wordlessly, he extended a gloved hand, not with the palm facing upward, but to shake mine. Without thinking I put my hand in his and we greeted each other in silence. I shook firmly – it made me feel good about myself to do that. Also, I remembered that he hadn't shaken hands with the other people and I was flattered that he had chosen me. His acceptance of me and the fact that I had passed some test he had set made me feel smug. I smiled because the moment was awkward, and when I did, he took a half-step towards me, threw his eyes up the platform furtively, then whispered out of the corner of his mouth, still holding my hand, 'How do you get out of this place?'

Irish, of course. Always, in this town. He spoke like an inmate in a POW film, casting an eye around to see if the guards had noticed. The effect was almost funny. It might have been the furtive manner in which he delivered the question, but I was completely thrown by it. I hadn't the faintest idea what he meant. Maybe I was thrown because he hadn't asked me for money. I had been prepared to tell him I had none on me (which happened to be the truth) but I was thrown too because the exit was so clearly marked at the end of the platform.

'This place?' It was all I could manage, pointing a finger down at the litter-strewn concrete of the platform.

'Yeah, this place. How do you get out of here?'

He let go of my hand and threw his arms open wide as if to say, 'The station. The neighbourhood. The entire *system*!' Maybe he was referring to England.

Then he let his hands drop to his sides and his shoulders slumped, exhausted by the effort. I leaned forward to share his point of view, then I cast an eye up the platform. I pointed out the exit at the far end of the platform to him. It was clearly marked but maybe he was blind. He narrowed his eyes at me. He was neither blind nor deaf.

'Where in Ireland are you from?'

Nobody has heard of my suburb, so I mentioned the one nearest to where I grew up.

'Is that where the mental hospital is?'

It is. He gave a crooked smile. He was managing to slag me off for growing up where I had, and as soon as I acknowledged the joke with a smile of my own, his smile dropped.

'Are you a smackhead?'

'No.'

'Do you do smack?'

'No.'

'You wouldn't make it in Moss Side. Do you know what they'd do to you in Moss Side? He drew a gloved finger across his throat. Then he leaned in and hissed in my face. 'They'd cut your throat open and they'd leave you to die.'

Now I take a step back. My train rolls into view behind him as he steps forward, grabs my hand and shakes it once again. This time I'm not shaking his hand as firmly. He quits the shake and steps away. The train doors open and it's not my train but I make to walk on anyway. From five paces off he turns around and aims his index fingers at me like a gun. 'Mind yourself.'

He smiles again and I board the train, then I smile back as the train doors close between us. I do. I do mind myself.

(First published in The Irish Times*)*

World Peace

Siobhán Donohue, Bray, County Wicklow

She lies beside me in the bed, sleeping. Her breathing is silent but I can see the gentle rise and fall of her chest. Her shapely head is bald save for a smattering of fluffy fair hair. Her perfect ears lie neatly against the side of her head. Pale pink-purple eyelids below barely visible blonde eyebrows end in long, dark lashes. Her button nose is ever so slightly turned up and her pink lips perfectly frame her small mouth. She is peaceful and she is perfect and I am smitten.

She stirs, eyelids flickering and head turning to the side so that she faces me. I lie still, willing her not to open her eyes just yet so that I may continue to observe her unnoticed. She grimaces and she wrinkles her high forehead as if dreaming. She turns back to face the ceiling. She lifts her arms above her head and stretches, arching her back, lifting her chin and pouting her lips. The stretch ends and her eyes open fully. She gazes at the ceiling, flapping her hands and flexing her toes as she focuses on the lampshade hanging above her head. It makes her smile.

She has no awareness of recession or credit crunch, of NAMA or the untimely death of our Celtic Tiger. She knows nothing of unrest in Afghanistan or Iraq or of the war on terror since that September day. She worries not about finding a job or paying a mortgage. She doesn't spend hours wondering what she will do with her life or where she will meet the man of her dreams. She is unaware of climate change, global warming, famine or starving children. She has no political views or anger about government policy and no desire to join protest marches to Government Buildings.

She does know that she gets hungry and that drinking her milk makes her feel better. She knows she likes to be held in warm, strong arms that make her feel safe. She knows her mum and dad and that her two-year-old brother makes her laugh. She knows she feels better when she burps and she somehow knows it is good to stretch.

She turns her head and faces me again. This time her bright, clear, blue eyes meet mine and I am discovered. I am rewarded by an open-mouthed smile that spreads to those beautiful eyes and with happy cooing and chuckling and excited movement of limbs. I cannot help but smile back. Images begin to flash through my mind, snapshots from the future. I imagine what her voice will sound like when she begins to talk. I see her running in the garden, her brother chasing her. I picture her the first time she goes swimming and her surprise and excitement when she first experiences snow.

But for now I am happy to share simple, happy smiles with her and make faces and funny noises to make her smile again. And in that moment, there is no credit crunch, no war, no famine or any other problem in the world. There is just me and Aoife, my beautiful baby girl.

Froggy

Maura Melia, Kilsaran, County Louth

It was 1973. I was nineteen. I was playing with a dance band in a hotel on Achill Island. We were unique in that we had two females – one on vocals and myself on keyboard. While the lads were setting up the gear, we adjourned to the lounge to have a drink. Two Frenchmen came over and started talking to us. I was very happy to use my Leaving Certificate French and enjoyed the conversation. They came to the dance and one of them came up to the stage frequently to smile, talk and leave me a drink – orange juice.

When the dance was over he came up and we started talking again. The band was staying over in the hotel so we arranged to go for a walk the next day. (That's what you did in those days.) We talked and talked and exchanged addresses. He was travelling around Ireland and I was moving on to Sligo for our next gig. I doubted if I would ever hear from him again – but I did! About a month later I received a letter from France and replied. His name was Christian – and since I had difficulty with the guttural 'r' I called him Froggy. Since he had a similar difficulty he called me Paddy. We exchanged letters for a year. I wrote in English and he wrote in French. We got to know each other at a soul level. A very deep bond developed.

We planned a holiday together in Ireland during the following summer. On the date of his arrival my parents drove me to the airport to collect him. I was filled with anxiety. Would I recognise him? Would we be able to talk as we had done? We were in new territory, so far advanced from our casual meeting of the previous year. I stood in the arrivals' area, my eyes on stalks, waiting for him. But somehow I missed him. I was becoming anxious when I heard a voice behind me, 'Hello, Paddy!' There he was. I was caught in his arms and I hugged him. And if my parents were watching, that was OK too. We drove home, my parents making conversation and we in the back seat giggling and talking in French. He had brought a silk scarf for my mother and cognac for my dad – who was a lifelong Pioneer. I got perfume and a Waterman pen set, which I still cherish.

I still had a week to go before my holidays so each evening he would get the bus into town to meet me after work. I danced out each day, knowing he was waiting for me on the footpath. We would go for coffee, then get the bus home. Mum made a real effort to serve up haute cuisine in his honour. Dad took him to meet the local Scouts. Froggy was involved with the Scouts in France and Dad was the unit leader with the local troop. They were going camping to France the following month and Froggy arranged to meet up with them when they arrived.

We planned to tour Ireland together. By this time I had left the band. We decided to start our tour in the place we had first met so we travelled to Achill, a year from the day we first met. What a surprise awaited us. My former bandmates were playing in the hotel that night! We went in and had a surprise reunion. Froggy and I danced all night – the only time in my life that I have been able to jive. We seemed to be connected on an energy level. I was tossed and caught, under his leg, over his shoulder, in front, behind, totally free and in tune with him. So much so that the crowd formed a circle round us to watch. It was the stuff of fairytales, a wonderful, magical experience.

Next morning we set off for Kerry. We toured the Ring, enjoying the shopping, cooking and eating. We hitch-hiked through the south, my hand in his back pocket and his arm around my shoulders. We sang songs. I taught him Irish songs – like 'Four Green Fields' – and he taught me French songs. I can still remember most of:

Monsieur Le Président,
Je vous écris une lettre,
Que vous lirez, peut être,
Si vous avez le temps...

From Kerry we travelled to west Cork and on to Cape Clear, a beautiful 'other world'. We went to Garnish Island and it felt like the Taj Mahal to be there with someone you loved and who loved you.

Then it was Wicklow, Glendalough, Dublin. We went to Trinity College to see *The Book of Kells*. We went into the canteen to eat. They had a wonderful menu with many options for each course, all of which included Potage du Jour. We should have copped it! We ordered our individual choices but both received the aforementioned 'Potage du Jour', the only item on the menu! We crossed town and sat in the Garden of Remembrance. I told him the story and we sat in silence, each of us honouring our own. And honouring each other.

Those three weeks were filled with laughter, wonder, dreams and joy at seeing my country through the eyes of another. We planned how it would be when I travelled to France at Christmas. He encouraged me to role-play: going shopping, ordering a meal, introducing myself, meeting his family.

All too soon, it was time for him to return home. My parents had gone to Spain on holidays so we got the train to Dublin, then the bus to the airport. We went through the check-in procedures. Finally, he had to go through and I was left alone. At that time it was possible to see the passengers as they boarded the aircraft. I stood at the window, tears coursing down my face. I watched him climb the steps, turn and wave and disappear. I went out and got a taxi into Dublin. I couldn't stop the tears and wished the driver would stop trying to make conversation. I got on to the train and cried the whole way home.

I wrote to him that evening, telling him how much I missed him already but how much I was looking forward to seeing him again at Christmas. Letters from France took three days to arrive so I knew I would not hear from him for a while. I wrote again the next day. And the next. I began to wonder after four days. I wrote for several weeks, begging him to tell me he was OK. To explain what was happening. I began to wonder was my mother hiding the letters. Had he had an accident? The local Scouts went, as planned, to France. And he did meet them as arranged. It was very fortunate as he was able to bring a Scout who had been injured to hospital. But I never heard from him again.

The following year I was travelling to Galway with friends. On the road outside Mullingar I spotted a hitch-hiker. I don't know for certain but I'm fairly sure it was him. I was in shock and didn't say anything. We drove on. Maybe if we had stopped I would have answers. But I don't. And life goes on....

Michael and Eileen

Andrew Shiels, Cork

When we lived on the west coast of Ireland, we used to buy milk from a small farm. Fresh from the udder, collected in an old enamel pitcher, it tasted wonderful – none of today's homogenised, chill-sterilised, safe-to-drinkalised stuff. This was whole milk from an old-fashioned cow, drawn in the traditional way and much the better for it.

Our house had a couple of acres of grass and Michael, the farmer, would come over with his scythe in June to cut the long sward for hay. He would work for hours, swishing the blade back and forth. From time to time the scrape of sharpening stone on metal would punctuate the quiet of the sea breeze. As the day warmed, the fragrant perfume of fallen grass intensified, while drying leaf and stem shrank back. Michael would toil on, carefully economic in his work. The rhythmic elegance of his scythe's movement would have been the envy of many a golfer.

He was one of the most contented people I had ever encountered. Although he was bent-over old and with knuckles swollen and arthritic, his face always had a smile. I could hardly understand a word he said in his broad country accent, let alone a sentence, but we seemed to get along just fine. When he stopped for a break, he would sit at the edge of the field, drinking cold tea from a bottle. I often invited him over to the house, to sit in the cool shade and eat his lunch, but he never came.

Once all the hay was cut, Michael would call over almost every day to check the crop. Rain was the biggest enemy but I never remember the hay being spoiled. He would walk along through the drying grass with a two-pronged pitch-fork, tossing the fallen stems in the breeze to hasten their drying. Depending on the weather, this could go on for anything up to a week, before he arrived with his donkey and cart to transport the crop home. I liked the idea that the cows giving us milk would feed on hay from our fields.

Sometimes I would go fishing in the afternoon. Down on the rocks I could sit for hours, watching the sea gently rise and fall, catching an occasional fish and relaxing in the solitude. The fish could be quite big but tasted awful and only our neighbour's cat would eat them. One day when I reached the top of the cliff path, Michael was there and called to me. I showed him the fish and his face shone more brightly than usual. Apparently he shared that cats' taste and from then on I would always give my catch to him.

His wife Eileen's taste in food was unknown to me but from the look of the cooking apparatus in their small house, the menu must have been limited. Suspended from a blackened chain, over an always-lit turf fire in the open hearth, hung a large cauldron. I never saw anything being cooked in it but always assumed that this was their cooking pot. Although I knew nothing of Eileen's cooking style, I soon learned of her passion for drink. Michael didn't touch spirits but there was always a bottle of whiskey open in the kitchen.

One memorable day my father came with me to collect the milk. Eileen hadn't seen him for some time and this appeared to her a great opportunity for celebration. She offered us a 'drop', which we were too polite to refuse, even if it was only ten in the morning. She placed a large glass on the table before each of us and half-filled both with the spirit, giving herself the same measure. My father and I had enough whiskey to drink her health a thousand times and the fiery liquid burned my throat.

When Michael came in with the milk we made a quick exit before the glasses could be refreshed.

Some time later we sold our house on the west coast and moved inland, losing touch with Michael and Eileen and resorting to supermarket milk. Several years later I heard that in the end, it was her drinking that did for poor old Michael. I had always assumed that the land belonged to him but it was her family's farm. When milk prices dropped, whiskey prices didn't follow and their income could no longer support Eileen's craving. So she took off into town on the weekly bus, put the farm on the market and had the place sold within a year.

Michael was devastated. Farming in his simple, yet effective way was all he had ever known and she had taken everything from him. They found him hanging in the cowshed. No suicide note – he had never learned to write.

I drove out that way a couple of years ago. The house was almost gone. The walls were crumbling and the roof timbers were rotting, exposed to the Atlantic gales. I don't think I will travel that road again.

Shallow Grave

Mary Sheehan, Dunmore East, County Waterford

'There's a grave in your field,' Percy blurted out and watched my mother's consternation as she sank on to a chair. He had the presence of mind to fill a glass with water from the kitchen tap and hand it to her. When she had revived somewhat she asked, 'Are you sure?' The glass was shaking in her hand.

'It looks like it and, well, you haven't lost any animals recently, have you?' Percy said. He was referring to the small flock of sheep, two ponies, and the various dogs and cats we had.

'No, not a one,' my mother replied.

'I didn't think so.' Percy was our nearest neighbour and he didn't miss a thing. It was reassuring to have such a vigilant neighbour.

'There's no other likely explanation. If it's not one of your animals then it must be a human buried there!'

His words hung in the air. It was the hiss of water on flames that eventually brought my mother back to earth. She had been cooking dinner when Percy walked in. The water was bubbling over from the potatoes. She went to turn down the gas and then with a determined twist she turned it off completely.

'I had better take a look,' she said, straightening up. It would be almost half an hour before my brothers and I would be home. Her curiosity would not allow her to wait that long to solve the mystery.

'I'll go get a shovel too,' Percy said as he left. My mother went to look for our own shovel and by the time she had tracked it down, hiding in a bunch of nettles out the back, Percy had returned. He had brought his daughter and her husband with him for moral support. This little group proceeded up the fields behind our house and Percy's. They were joined by our spaniels Nellie and Lassie, with Mrs Dunphy the cat bringing up the rear.

As they walked, the conversation centred on the story of a girl who was missing from the Woodstown area and presumed dead. It was top of the local news. Such events were rare enough in the early 1980s and were extremely shocking. Then there was the spate of local robberies: the creamery had been broken into twice in the previous month alone. What was the world coming to! A silence fell as they walked through the long summer grass; even the dogs were subdued, sensing the tension in the air.

Their shoes were damp and flecked with hayseed by the time they reached the back field. Percy led the way to the far corner. Because of the long grass they were upon the grave before they knew it. My mother instinctively took a step back.

The disturbed earth measured about two feet wide and six feet long. It wasn't freshly dug, judging by the small weeds and grass that were recolonising the earth. It looked to be a few weeks old. This was good, because the girl from Woodstown had been missing only a week. It mightn't be a grave at all. My mother held on to this thought as she pushed the shovel into the earth and with the practised ease that came from potato growing, she dug the first shovel full and upended the earth onto the grass.

Percy wiped the sweat from his brow. It was hot work on this sultry afternoon. They had dug down nearly a foot and found nothing. Then they realised that the reason why it was getting harder was not because they were tiring but because they were now digging undisturbed earth. The grave was only a foot deep! They looked at each other, puzzled and at the same time relieved.

'I was wondering why the dogs showed no interest in the grave,' my mother said, leaning on her shovel.

'True,' ventured Percy's daughter

'It would have been a weird place anyway to bury a body,' her husband chimed in. 'Who'd carry a body all the way up here to bury it. Makes no sense.'

My mother said nothing. She couldn't fathom it and was quite disturbed by the whole affair.

Percy voiced her thoughts.

'Well, it's still a mystery as to what the hell it is!'

That was the summer of 1981. Despite the economic recession that was swamping Ireland it was a vibrant time in our area, or maybe that is how I see it because I was sweet sixteen at the time. Either way, a lot of the old sports days and patterns were being revived in our local community, fundraising events to help to build a community centre. Everyone got involved and soon the roads were busy as people, young and old, started walking and running to get fit.

There was no great interest in sport in our house. My brothers were more interested in motorbikes than in footballs. But even we became caught up in the sporting atmosphere. My brother Chris started training for the local tug-of-war team. Soon the mantelpiece was chock-a-block with trophies, from small wooden pieces to huge marble and chrome things.

I added two dust collectors to the mantelpiece when I achieved my childhood ambition of becoming a successful jockey, albeit in two local donkey derbies. My mother added another trophy for her participation in the ladies' tug-of-war team. And even Lassie managed to secure a trophy in the Ballymacaw sports day!

Lassie was now leading the puzzled and weary group back home. My brothers had arrived home by this time and were wondering where dinner was. They were out of luck because the potatoes had gone to mush and the meat was burned to a cinder in the oven that my mother had forgotten to turn off.

With much drama my mother regaled my brothers with the

events of the afternoon. Chris was intrigued and had a theory that the shallow grave was in preparation for a murder. This was a new angle on the whole affair and left my mother lost for words.

My eldest brother David was also silent but for a different reason. He knew the truth...

David's contributions to the mantelpiece were trophies for the 100-metre sprint and the long jump. His training for the latter involved digging a practice jump in a quiet corner of a field where he would disturb no one. It wasn't exactly a secret: he just didn't see the need to tell anyone.

Dis-ease

Mary Clare O'Brien, Greystones, County Wicklow

The woman in blue from Reception showed me to Room 306 on the third floor. It was tiny, with space only for a small bed, a plastic chair and a sink. A long narrow window let in whatever light was left in the evening sun. I sat on the bed. It creaked and I started to slide off. I caught myself just in time and resumed standing as the woman in blue backed out the door.

'There'll be someone along to see you shortly. Good luck.'

Luck. Was that what had brought me to a maternity hospital to have a cancerous uterus removed? No, don't think, not now. To find out why I had slid off the creaky bed, I lifted the faded pink candlewick bedspread, then the blanket and the sheets. The mattress was covered in dark-blue plastic. I put the bedclothes back and practised sitting on the bed. If I placed my bottom in the middle, I didn't slide off. I leaned back against the pillow. It creaked. More blue plastic. The room was hot so I pushed up the bottom of the sash window. It moved only six inches before it met resistance. No chance of escaping that way.

I sat on the brown plastic chair. The walls were sick green, the door and window frame a dark wood. The floor was perhaps once fawn, with flecks of green. A white patch looked as if a cleaner had been over-zealous with bleach.

The door opened.

'Hi, I'm your surgeon. Sit up on the bed for me,' he ordered.

I was careful to sit in the middle. Creak.

'Lie back, please.'

I obeyed. Creak. He put his hands on my stomach and his fingers probed like radio antennae sweeping the heavens in search of alien life. Would he find it? Maybe it wasn't there at all. Maybe I was in the middle of a nightmare. He said nothing and never once looked at my face. Eyes were not important here. No one cared about them, even when they filled with tears. Stop. Don't.

'I'll see you at noon tomorrow,' he said and turned his back.

'Thank you,' I offered but he was gone.

I slid off the bed and grabbed the chair to prevent a hard landing. The room was even hotter now. Somewhere below gates whined, an engine revved, gates whined again and then clanged shut. My door opened. Does no one knock around here?

'Are you all right?' a nurse asked. No, I'm not all right. I'm in a cell and I may be dying. I want you to hold my hand and tell me I'm going to be all right, that this will all go away and that I won't die. And please take the plastic off the mattress and pillow. And bring me a fan.

'I'm fine, thank you, nurse,' I replied.

'I'm going off duty now but I'll see you in the morning.'

I lay awake all night, listening to the plastic creaking as I twisted and turned, getting hotter and hotter. If I opened the window, the noise of the city thundered in like a train in a tunnel. I opened the door and went out into the darkness of the silent corridor, with its six closed doors on one side and two high windows like mine on the other. As I walked up and down, I was so tired I could have been sleepwalking. I went back to my plastic bed and closed my eyes but immediately they flew open again. No. Don't think. You mustn't think. If you do, your heart will stop and you'll die of fear. I walked again along the cool corridor and thought of the yellow furze on the little Leitrim hills and the mist swirling around the regal swans on Lough Bran. Will I ever see my soul's solace again?

At exactly noon the following day, I was transferred to a trolley and wheeled into a room crowded with people in masks, strangers to whom I had handed over control of my body. And my life. Someone inserted a needle into my arm. When I awoke, I was back in my creaky bed in my airless cell, rigged up with oxygen and a morphine drip. A nurse placed a button in my hand and told me to press every twenty minutes for a shot of painkiller. I resolved to hold off on some presses, in case it ran out too soon. How was I to know that after twenty-four hours they would take out the drip, no matter how much morphine was left.

I fell into a deep sleep and awoke in the middle of the night, sweating. When I tried to move, I couldn't. My God, I'm paralysed. I tried to call out but no sound came. Now my voice is gone. I am dying bit by bit. My arms still worked so I groped for the call-bell and pressed. But no one came. Please, please, please. I pressed again. Nothing. I can't breathe. I'm going to die. Oh, somebody, please help me. After what seemed like a very long time of screaming silently, a Filipina nurse appeared.

'Are you OK?'

'No, no, no.' This time I said it out loud. 'I can't move. I'm dying. Please help me.'

I felt her cool hand on my forehead. Then she reached over to the sink, ran the tap on my facecloth, squeezed it and gently wiped my face and then my hands. And I wept.

'You must not cry, Mary,' she said in accented English. 'You will be all right. You are not paralysed and you are not dying. You have had a panic attack.'

How could I explain to her that my tears, at long last flowing, were not from fear but because of her kindness? This girl, so far from her home, will never know how much she meant to me that night, how her hands and voice and the cool of that facecloth soothed my terror.

Next day, the surgeon came to the door. 'You'll be perfectly fine from now on, Ms O'Brien. I've taken away all the cancer so you will be going home in a few days,' he said brusquely.

I wanted to kiss him but wisely restrained myself. Ever since the diagnosis, four weeks before, fear had been walking beside me as I had tried to put one foot in front of another, my mouth so dry I couldn't swallow and a lump in my throat that felt like my heart. Now I was alone again. I felt like singing

Five days later, I was preparing to go home when there was a rare knock on the door.

'Come in.'

It was the surgeon. Knocking? He sat on the bed. I noted he didn't slide off so I concluded that, through practice, he had mastered the art. His voice was quieter than usual, gentle even, as he uttered the words he had persuaded me I would not hear.

'I'm sorry, I was wrong. The cancer was more advanced than I thought.' He said something else but I didn't hear. There was someone screaming and I was falling into a deep dark hole where I could see nothing. Gradually my eyes adjusted and I saw a shadow coming towards me. I turned to run but there was nowhere to go. Slowly, as I forced myself to look at it, the horror revealed itself. As it did, it also started to dissolve and the darkness began to lift.

In Room 306, the surgeon had been replaced by a nurse.

'Now, Mary, don't worry, you'll be fine. I'll be setting up all your appointments for chemotherapy and radiotherapy and in a few months you'll be as right as rain. For now, just go home and gather your strength. Come, I'll help you pack. I'm sure you're dying to get out of here.'

She didn't appear to get her own joke. I did but it wasn't funny. It is now, because I didn't die. One long year later, I am as right as rain, as she promised.

With It Come Darkness and Peace

Emer Davis, Shankill, County Dublin (originally Achill)

I was fifteen years old in the early 1980s when my mother introduced me to *Madame Butterfly*, the same age as Butterfly when she met Pinkerton, the American naval officer. I sat in front of the old black-and-white television watching her guiding her girlfriends into the garden. Every Christmas and Easter we were immersed in the world of opera and ballet in our small rural sitting room. While our friends milked cows, sang in the local church choir and covered their love bites with polo necks and woollen scarves we wallowed in RTE's bi-annual display of high art.

My love affair with this opera began when I listened to 'One More Step' and Butterfly pointed out her future husband. From that moment I knew her love was doomed and like her I succumbed to Pinkerton's charm and effortless affection. I was blinded by his worldliness. My innocence was eroded with each aria. After the 'Humming Chorus', when Butterfly, her child and her maid Suzuki waited all night for Pinkerton, I cried with her when she realised he wasn't coming for her.

Several years later, as a student in Dublin, I came across a double album of *Madame Butterfly*. Its sumptuous cover of oriental mysteries, white petals, frosted buds and hand-painted fans left a lasting impression on me. Remembering the simple words of 'Night is Falling', I paid over the £8 and walked out with a memory of Butterfly singing, 'With It Come Darkness and Peace.' I didn't own a record player at the time.

In a friend's house I took the record out of its sleeve and placed it on the turntable, cautiously letting the needle down on to its groove. Alone I listened to the sound fill the room. Glad to miss a night out in the local pub, I chose to stay behind and hear the murmur of hushed voices reverberating in the small terraced house. Familiar sounds from my childhood replayed after a long absence. My hour. For six months I relived this moment, allowing these delicate voices to seep into my veins, tripping me up. I was hooked.

The years rolled on and after some time away from Ireland and *Butterfly* I returned home and met my future husband who shared my passion for this tragic heroine. We travelled to Italy, visiting Rome, Sorrento, Capri, Naples, Florence and Asiago. In Florence we went for a meal in a restaurant off one of the narrow side streets leading to the Arno. It was a small intimate place, with dark wood, simple furnishings and fresh food. Sipping wine I found myself idly humming along to a duet straying from the speaker. It was vaguely familiar. A ring appeared in front of me. I heard his voice interrupting the 'Love Me Please' aria and a hush descended among the crowd. Faces turned towards me, waiting for my answer. Cheers rang through the room as I took his hand.

Earlier this year I booked four tickets online for *Madame Butterfly* in the National Concert Hall and printed the tickets off, storing them in my handbag. I never checked them. It was the day before my mother's anniversary Mass. Five years on the memories were still as strong. On Saturday 20 February we made our way to the Concert Hall. Someone else was sitting in our seats. We both produced our tickets. I looked at the day and date. It was for the following night. We walked out. After explaining to the manager what happened we were given better seats in the yellow balcony and I felt my mother was watching with me.

I am not one for standing at gravesides, looking at slabs

of stone. I find my mother is always with me when I look at a painting, hear a piece of music, walk along a beach or browse in second-hand bookshops. She was with me that night and I could see her watching that old black and white television with *The Irish Times* folded in one hand and a cigarette in the other.

A Marriage of Inconvenience

Quentin Fottrell, Dublin

The website made it seem as if I was signing up to something wonderful and dangerous, like a high-interest platinum credit card that promised discounts on fabulous hotels and first dibs on theatre tickets, or a service for finding a mail-order bride. This was actually my last task as a card-carrying member of the Roman Catholic Church. All I had to do was log on to countmeout.ie, roll my mouse over the royal blue button that said 'Click Here To Begin!', plug in my details and send it off. I would be silently removed from the Church register forever.

If I did this I wouldn't be buried in a Catholic churchyard but I think I can live with that. I wouldn't be married in a Catholic Church but this was never going to happen, anyway – not if I was standing shoulder-to-shoulder with another man.

I felt sad. The Church and I have had a lot of adventures together. As an altar boy, I once got a fit of the giggles during Mass as I waved at friends in the congregation. The priest stomped backstage. 'If you do that again,' he said, 'you will be banned from the Sacristy.' I went home and looked up 'Sacristy' in the dictionary. I immediately understood. Any more funny business and he would fire me…from a job that didn't even pay. I wanted out of my black-and-white vestments but not this way. I served Mass for another couple of weeks silently and respectfully. Then, when he least expected it, I walked.

This time, I was walking away from the whole kit and kaboodle. I had seen and heard enough.

Psychologically, I would be free.

My First Communion and Confirmation, those two milestones on the road to becoming a fully-fledged member of the Church, were less than successful, and perhaps signs that my parents were trying to fit a square peg (that would be me) into a round hole (the Church).

My Communion outfit was a white v-neck jumper with a navy nylon polo-neck underneath, heavy navy wool flares and blue round-toed shoes with a buckle. I looked like a bad Val Doonican album cover. Or Americana Honeymoon Chic.

We bought my ensemble in the old Dundrum Shopping Centre. Before Harvey Nichols and H&M there were Quinnsworth and Sibley's. Sibley's sold Papermate and Parker pens. To celebrate this special day, I was given a Parker. It came in a smart coffin-like box lined in felt.

The trousers were the last item to be chosen and the most controversial. The wool irritated my skin horribly. 'They feel all scratchy,' I protested.

'They won't itch when you go out into the fresh air,' my mother said.

I didn't know how to answer that. She had me on a technicality: I couldn't test her theory in the shop. I was out-maneouvered. When I went home, I put the trousers on, went out into the garden to let the fresh air work their magic…but they still itched like crazy. Ants in my pants would be the least of my worries on my Communion Day.

I changed trousers and spent the rest of the afternoon playing with my next-door neighbour's orange hoola-hoop. I jostled and swung and twirled it for hours and again on the morning of my First Communion.

It was a beautiful day. My older sister Alison insisted on coming along for 'the meal' afterwards. We didn't eat out much in those days so the prospect of going somewhere vaguely swanky like the Royal Hotel in Bray was a treat. I was the youngest of five – hence my name, with three older sisters and one older brother – and one of my sisters had nabbed a seat at the table. She had black hair just below her shoulders, with dramatic and threatening blow-dried wings on each side. You could still see the comb marks. If I acted the maggot, she would make me pay. As it turned out, I would get more than my share of the spotlight…thanks to the hoola-hoop.

We had just started our lunch when I complained about feeling sick. This was a bad development so early in the day. I had only five pounds in my pocket and this didn't bode well for earning more money. 'Don't mind him,' Alison said, 'he's only looking for attention.'

The words were barely out of her mouth when I vomited violently all over the table.

I don't remember much else except lingering on the edge of consciousness and being carried into the back of my father's Ford Cortina. The hoola-hoop had activated my dormant kidney stones. I was born with them and they were embedded deep in my organs like little time bombs, waiting for their chance to go off. Years later, my guilt-ridden sister described the scene. Alison recalled me asking my parents, 'Am I going to die?' My poor folks probably hadn't even thought of that…until I brought it up. If I was a Bride of Christ and didn't want to go through with it, I could just have come down with a headache.

There were no wardrobe or hoola-hoop malfunctions with my Confirmation. No siblings were invited along to 'the meal' this time. This day out was for me alone. We were back at 7pm sharp. No visiting relatives or neighbours. No amateur dramatics. No Exorcist moment over lunch. No rushing to hospitals. No bells. No whistles.

There was a reason for the scaled-down version of my big day. The previous Sunday, after Mass at the Good Shepherd in

Churchtown, a neighbour, Mrs Nicholson, asked me, 'Are you looking forward to it?'

My mother beamed. She had done a lot of planning.

'Not particularly,' I replied.

There followed a long silence. 'Oh...' Mrs Nicholson said. Her smile lingered precariously on her face but it was now just a technicality.

My mother's face was impassive. It was much harder to read.

We got into the car without a word. My mother slammed the door shut. That was not a good sign. The Ford Cortina was long gone. This time we drove a white Mercedes. That car caused quite a stir when my father bought it. The catty remarks by neighbours' kids taught me something: you should never look too pleased with yourself while swanning around in a white Mercedes in the 1980s. Which was just as well: one week before my Confirmation, on this sunny Sunday morning, neither of us had anything to smile about.

'Not particularly?' my mother said, as she drove out of the church gates and changed gears with an angry click and a thump. 'Not particularly! Not particularly!' my mother said again and again, compressing me into a contrite and petrified silence. I had blown it. There would be no Parker pen from Sibley's for me. Not even a Papermate. Whatever credit I had in the bank to make up for being hospitalised on the day of my First Communion was long gone.

I didn't have an ugly Confirmation suit run up by a neighbour on a spinning Jenny. I wore my new de La Salle school uniform: black blazer, white shirt, black tie with gold crest, matching black shoes and grey flannel trousers. And a rosette. No dodgy album covers this time around.

The bishop called out the names I had chosen. I picked three and would have chosen a fourth if I could have squeezed it on the form. My full name would now read: 'Quentin Joseph

Patrick Daniel Guy Fottrell.' Patrick because it was Irish. Daniel because I thought of it as Anglo-American wholesome-butch. Guy because he was Tarzan's friend in the TV series and I figured no one else would choose it. (I was right.) When I rejoined my parents in the pew after being confirmed my brother Henry whispered in my ear: 'You do know that when the bishop read out your names the whole church burst out laughing at you!' At least my big moment hadn't gone unnoticed. This time my parents brought me to Killiney Castle for 'the meal', followed by a swim in the pool. Then it was straight home.

My mother, of course, looked beautiful in an aquamarine silk dress, and had not held anything against me: it was merely 7pm and time to go home. But I needed a conspiracy theory on my Confirmation day. Drama was like mother's milk to me and I whined all the way to our house.

All of that was a long time ago. I finally printed out the letter from countmeout.ie and posted it. It was a bit like getting divorced after a bad marriage. I didn't leave because of these experiences but they did tell me something about my relationship with the Church. Perhaps they were early-warning signs that it was never going to work. I had giggled my way through Mass, vomited over my First Communion lunch and turned my nose up at my Confirmation. If the Archdiocese of Dublin calls to ask if I want to stay in the Church, I will simply refer them to my earlier statement, given to Mrs Nicholson on the steps of the Good Shepherd.

I will also have to kiss goodbye to Patrick, Daniel and Guy, my three imaginary ex-husbands. I will miss them most of all.

Nanny to the Rescue

Mary Dunne, Ballymoneen, Avoca, County Wicklow

It was a sunny Saturday morning in April 2007. I was caring for my three grandchildren. They were playing in the back garden, I was peeling potatoes at the kitchen sink when suddenly I looked out to check on them and I heard shouting under the trees. They were looking up.

Oh no, I don't believe it. A mane of blonde hair hanging from the top of the tallest tree. Paddy, aged three, came running. 'Nanny, Roisin is stuck up the big tree.'

I took two jumps on to the ditch under the tree. Roisin, also aged three, was at the very top. 'Nanny, my arms are getting tired.'

'Hang on, you'll be OK, I'll get to you, I'll get to you.'

My heart was racing. What was I going to do? An old woman in her dressing gown, on her own, a child up a tree, two others crying with fright, the biggest of them, Aine, only seven. Paddy was shouting, 'We told you not to climb so high, but oh no, you had to keep going. You were just showing off. Now see what has happened.'

I could just see Roisin's shoe through the branches of the high evergreen, I'm terrified of heights but here goes, I'll have to try. The branches keep breaking and scratching my bony legs. I can almost reach her shoe, all the time calling to her, 'Don't let go, you must hold on.'

As I looked down to the two little ones staring at me I nearly died of fright, I was never going to get down. Now the two of us were stuck.

'Aine, you will have to help me. Go in and get the phone, dial 999 and tell the man your nanny and cousin are stuck up a big tree, please come to the rescue.'

'OK, Nanny, 999. If they want to know where we live, what will I say?'

'No, wait, Aine, hang up. If your grandad comes home and sees the fire brigade in the yard, he'll have a heart attack.'

So taking my life in my hands I climbed further until I had my arm around Roisin's shoulder. 'Now you must listen to me. Very slowly. We'll make it together.' So we started our descent, It took us about ten minutes to reach the ground.

My legs were torn and scratched and my arms covered in splinters, as were Roisin's.

When we relaxed after having ice-cream we had a good laugh about it. Aine asked, 'Nanny, if the fire brigade had come would the fireman have blasted you and Roisin down from the tree with his big water hose?

Bean Sídhe

Pól Mac Reannacháin, Strabane, County Tyrone

The road begins to cut through rust-red rock. That is its way of saying that you're approaching the coast of Donegal. After the placid green meadows around Lifford and Raphoe, the change to the rugged, volcanic vaults and towers of the coast is all the more striking. It is against this land that the Atlantic Ocean expends all its wrath. Rolling across thousands of miles of open sea, wind and wave plough the cliffs and sea-caves into tortured furrows. It is appropriate, then, that the ferry that links the mainland at Burtonport with Aranmore Island's main town of Leabgarrow is named *Misneach* – 'Courage'. The *Misneach*, red and white, a roll-on roll-off car ferry open to the air, picks out its hazardous route through a labyrinth of wrack-blackened islets, currents, eddies and submerged rocks, barnacle-encrusted like the snouts of whales, to dock at the simple concrete pier.

Aranmore ('Great Bread') is a soft green dome in the clear, summer tranquillity. When the sea lies still, murmuring against the white sands and black boulders of its coast, it looms out in sleepy benevolence. But the sea is deceitful, and many men have gone to sea from Leabgarrow never to return, swallowed up, some never found.

The house, old-fashioned, white-washed, compact and doughty in fields of tough grass and thistles, looks out over the quiet slopes of the island to the blue meridian of the Atlantic. Our stay of one week was prolonged by a gathering storm. Other visitors, backpackers from England, had been cycling around the island and were aiming to return to the mainland in their own boat. *The Misneach* was biding the storm in Burtonport harbour.

That night the gale thickened. Around the house the leaden air hammered against the island. A child at the time, tucked under a counterpane in a wrought-iron bed, I heard crying on the wind. Or was it only the wind singing? No, there again, carried on the wind rushing up from the sea, a woman keening. I shut my eyes and dared not move. What could that be outside the small, deep-set windows but the banshee? I did not want to see her. I did not want to hear her crying, a portent that someone was dying. Someone I knew.

The storm submitted to a sunny morning. A Sea King helicopter, bulbous and yellow, roared over the island. Looking from the sides of the *Misneach* as it threaded its way back amongst the islands, I could see small boats waiting for diverse shards of fibreglass to return from the black and silent sea. The backpackers' boat. They had gone out in that storm and the sea had destroyed them, hefted their frail vessel on to the hard sides of the rocks and shattered it. And they were dead. The sea had swallowed them too. The last of them was found by divers following the tracks made by scavenging crabs on the sea-bed.

At home the disaster made the news, not least because one of the storm's victims was the son of an official at Buckingham Palace. But no one mentioned the banshee. Only I knew about her. Only I had heard her. And I told no one. I pictured her in my mind, drifting in the black tide of the gale like a cobweb murmuring in a draught, her long hair uncoiling in the rushing air, as if it were she who were suspended underwater and not the one she cried for, her dark mourning weeds a membrane of squid ink bleeding out in the raging storm. And her cry: an anguished, sustained emptying of her grief, brought to the house, to my window, to me.

It is only now that I see the truth in that banshee's cry. It is only many years later that a fanciful childish mind seems preferable to the understanding of an adult. The banshee is the *bean sídhe*, the 'spirit woman'. She is a relic of the old gods, and mourns the passing of one whose ancestors used to revere her and her kind. It is only now, many years later, that I realise that the banshee did not cry for those drowned in that storm. Not because they were not the descendants of her worshippers. Not because she does not exist.

Now, many years later, I wish she did. I wish it was she I had heard that night. Because I did hear cries carried on the wind, cries carried up from the sea. They were cries proclaiming the death of people I knew – the backpackers encountered as they walked their bicycles down to the harbour.

Because they were their cries.

Lost in Translation

Jim Gargan, Cavan

How can I begin to describe this woman? If woman indeed she was, for I have my doubts. Imagine a crow, whose form was contorted and forced to take the shape of an old hag; that is what this woman put me in mind of. Her jet-black hair stood in thick plumes that shot from her scalp as if she'd been chewing on a power cable. Her eyes were dark and beady, adorned with horn-rimmed glasses sitting on the bridge of a broad nose that resolved itself in a fearsome hook. The lips were thin and pursed, like a grin turned upside down, above which was evidence of a moustache that, if left unchecked, would be worthy of any discerning gentleman. She wore the same clothes whenever I saw her, a black figure-hugging T-shirt and a black dress that came to just below her knees. She also wore sandals, the straps of which seemed to be biting into her swollen ankles. I presumed this to be the cause of her limp. Perhaps it is kindest to think of her as the antithesis of all that is beautiful.

She was my landlady for two months during the summer of 2001. I had just finished my second year in college and went to Germany for the summer to work for Audi in the town of Ingolstadt, about an hour from Munich. I can't remember her name...Frau Hellzeit is as good a name as any. She didn't speak a word of English and all I had in my armoury were the ghosts of Leaving Cert German, a random assortment of words at the best of times. This brief story is of my first encounter with Hellzeit and how even the blackest, most midnight hag can be made laugh...even if this was terrifying in itself.

It's possible that anyone reading this could mistake me for an ageist person, or some sort of sociopath, harbouring a grudge against this elderly woman. Nothing could be further from the truth: if anyone has reason to bear a grudge against Hellzeit, it's me. She stole from me, something that I could not prove at the time, but there is no one else it could have been. And it's not just that she stole: the object she purloined was irreplaceable. It was a ring, a gift from my father, that had come down father to son for three generations, back to my great-grandfather who had been chief of police in New York. It was his ring, a relic from another world with a beautiful engraving of a rainbow, representative of his division. The ring meant a lot to me and, to this day, I haven't plucked up the courage to tell my father that the line of the ring stopped with me.

It happened like this. Close to the end of my stay in Ingolstadt, I went travelling with a girl I'd met over there. Marianne was her name and we just hopped on a train without much of a notion and made our way to a lakeside town that was flanked by Austria on one side and Switzerland on the other. We had quite an interesting time, me and Marianne. The first night we arrived very late and had no choice but to set up our tent practically in the middle of the town roundabout – that's how organised we were. Did anything happen between me and the lovely Marianne? No, six years boarding in an all-boys' school left me somewhat shy, but I'd like to think something could have...**a** peck on the cheek at the very least. Anyway, towards the end of the week, Marianne had to get back and I was catching the ferry to Switzerland to do a bungee jump and white-water rafting.

For this very reason, I'd left the ring behind me in the absolute dump of a basement room Hellzeit was renting to me and my buddy Rob. I'd surely lose it doing a bungee or in the water so I thought it best to leave it behind, sitting atop my plane tickets on a locker right beside my bed. Imagine my surprise on my return when my key wouldn't work in the door of the room and there was no one to be seen anywhere.

There had been a breakdown in communication somewhere. I'd been gone longer than planned and my phone had died days before, as I hadn't brought the charger with me. There was nothing to be done but wander back into Ingolstadt and to find someone who could shine some light on this.

Eventually I met someone, for there was a strong Irish presence in the town. It was full of students like myself and we all knew one another. I got in touch with Rob and found that the demonic Hellzeit had evicted him in my absence and we were now living somewhere else. That's all fine and grand, I said, but where's my stuff? Rob didn't know.

I had to walk back out to the house to try to explain to her that my belongings were still in there: plane tickets, clothes, everything. I went back to her with the key and she casually told me that she had dumped anything left behind in the bin outside her house, the one I was standing beside right now. She also told me I could search it if I wanted, as she turned to go back inside.

So there I was, like a filthy tramp, searching through someone else's garbage and voilà, from the midst of the rotting banana skins and some seriously questionable pornographic magazines, I pulled my plane tickets and some books. I couldn't believe it. I was furious and despairing for there was no sign of the ring. I rang her door again and grilled her as best I could with my limited German but she maintained there had been no ring. What could I do? So with a heavy heart I turned and traipsed away. My only source of comfort is that she had to clean up her putrid, pornographic mess herself for I overturned the bin. Small victories count in my book. It had to have been her. She would have seen it on top of the tickets. Beady little crow's eyes like hers wouldn't miss a treasure like that.

She was a terror in other ways too. She didn't speak, she squawked. She didn't look, she gawked. One night, not long after we had moved in, she entered the room at about six in the morning. I was wide awake but I pretended to be asleep, yet I was watching from the corner of my eye. She sat down at the bottom of Rob's bed and just looked at him for a while, maybe about five minutes. Then she got up again and limped out again. I mean, what kind of a person does that? What the hell was she doing?

The day we first met was when she showed us the room and, having no other options, Rob and I decided to take it. It was far from cheerful, more the kind of room that made you want to cry, but it was cheap. So we sat down and negotiated the price. I had to do all the talking for Rob had no German, nor the slightest inclination towards learning any, so it was quite difficult, mostly, and I was thinking that this woman was a witch.

We hammered out the price eventually and the day the rent was to be collected and all that. Picture us in the dark, dingy room of her home, her sitting at the table, me sitting opposite her, Rob standing up behind me. To my surprise, she started to make small talk after the business end was done, asking me about Ireland, me replying as much as my limited German would allow. Then came the question: *Gibt es Krieg in Irland?* My thought process was as follows: *Krieg...Krieg...Krieg?* Ah yes, *Krieg* is Christ, or Mass, or something like that. She's asking me about religion, *Gibt es Krieg in Irland*. Is Ireland very religious?

Delighted with my linguistic ability I replied in the best German as I could muster: 'Yes, but these days *Krieg* isn't as important as it was. Most people, however, still go to *Krieg* every Sunday. It usually starts at about half past ten and lasts for about forty-five minutes.'

She threw back her oversized head and bellowed a great gust of laughter that almost knocked me out the window...and she continued to laugh for quite some time. I heard Rob behind me ask, 'What did you just say?' I had no idea.

I can't remember if it was she who explained or someone else, that *Krieg* means war. She had been asking about the Troubles in the North and was the war there over?

In my darkest dreams, I can still hear that hideous laughter.

A Tale, a Tale

Vanessa Delaney, Clontarf, Dublin

A tale, a tale have I. A tale of contemporary Ireland! I have many tales but I discard them all because the participants are still alive and may not want to be included in my scribbles. Still I cannot resist telling this tale of two tales, which is in essence true.

I think of a friend's girlfriend ten years ago, pregnant. A girl who had been told by her gynaecologist that she would probably never conceive. So when her parents heard their unmarried daughter's news, they celebrated and said what a great man he was and all sorts of other wonderful things that make a man grow about five inches! His parents were distinctly not of like mind with her parents at the time when, over a half-bottle of whiskey, I first heard the news of the imminent baby. His parents appeared to be ready to disown anything to do with his girlfriend and their grandchild. The young man was torn between protecting his girlfriend, now pregnant with their child, and maintaining what had up to then been a very close relationship with his warm and loving parents. Now he was being asked to question their values and it felt to him as if he had to choose whose side he was on. It just didn't seem right.

I told him a story that I held up to myself as an illustration of how best to behave in times when you want to say to your family, 'To hell with the lot of you'. Or something worse! Helped by a large glass of whiskey, I told him a story that promised him that if he ignored his parents' disgust and visited and telephoned them as normal, all would be well. When the child is born, all will be forgotten and there will be no grandparents more doting.

The story I told him was this:

It was around 1986 and we were at that age when we were falling one by one into settled relationships. Some of us had a few failed relationships under our belts. Some were sticking with the one man and heading straight for marriage. One friend, Gillian, wasn't so lucky. There was no more welcoming shoulder to cry on when you had a broken heart or were simply in need of comfort. But despite her warm and bubbly personality, Gillian didn't have a man of her own. Gillian was born with a large strawberry birthmark on the left side of her face and it seemed as if all too many people had to struggle to see beyond this. Nobody was more deserving of a good man than Gillian but the men were just not appearing.

Then one night, while they were out with friends, Gillian and Niall found themselves laughing and smiling in unison. They soon shared many laughs. Over the weeks and months that followed, we witnessed big, dirty laughs and also that warm laugh you hear when it is not so much that something is funny as that two people are plain happy together. And so everyone should have been happy, delighted, elated. Especially, Gillian's family. Their only daughter had found a good man.

But no, Gillian and Niall are from different religions and her family was horrified that she would even consider marrying outside her religion – even though the number of eligible males of her religion in Ireland can at best be described as seriously limited. Her extended family said things about Niall that are best not repeated. Horrible letters were sent from sisters-in-law with all sorts of threats. Gillian's mother didn't ring Gillian but Gillian did ring her mother and many phone calls ended in tears, although her mother would not always have been aware of Gillian's tears. There were long silences from her mother to Gillian. It went on and on. There was much hurt. There was much confusion. Gillian spoke openly and honestly to Niall about it all. He felt deeply for her and said that much as he loved her, he could never ask her to choose. Throughout this time, Gillian never missed a birthday or a family occasion. She sent birthday presents to her brothers, nieces and nephews as usual. She held her head high and rode slowly and painfully through it all.

Gradually her family realised that this guy was there to stay and gradually they were drawn to seeing him as the warm, loving man he is. The seeds of bitterness had been planted but when Gillian didn't water them, they withered and died. I remember the happy wedding as the father of the bride walked proudly down the aisle with his beautiful daughter.

And so it has come to pass for my whiskey-sharing friend and his wife, their two children and their doting grandparents.

Memories of My Father

Sarah Robertson, Greystones, County Wicklow

My father died suddenly in his mid-forties, a real loss to us, his family, and also to the rural community he lived in. My father had the biggest heart any one could possibly have. He personally felt everyone's pain and was always helping people in the community in any way he could. As a young child I remember my father coming home on Christmas day and crying for the people he had either delivered Christmas dinner to or brought to the community centre to have their Christmas dinner. He wished he could have brought them all home with him. Only for my mother I'd say he would have.

I remember that in the early 1980s one of my father's friends, a commandant in the army, went to the Lebanon for six months. My father, knowing his friend would be missing home, wrote to him as often as he could over those months. I remember being in the post office with my father buying special stamps for the defence forces stationed abroad. There were no mobile phones or internet in those days so apart from letters, army personnel was totally cut off.

My father died a few years after this and a lasting picture I have is of my father's friend in his uniform in full salute, staring straight ahead, standing on the steps at the back of the church as they carried my father's coffin past him. A fitting farewell.

The Making of an Imaginary Friend

Sylvia Petter, Vienna

When I first started writing, I went to Ireland with my husband to visit friends in Mulranny, County Mayo, hoping to see Heinrich Böll's cottage on Achill Island. It was closed to the public the day we drove by, so all I had was a view of a little white house behind a closed gate.

The next day golf was on the agenda. A fierce wind was blowing on the links near Belmullet and I opted to stay in the clubhouse in front of a warm open fire, nursing clam chowder and reading Edna O'Brien's biography of James Joyce. I don't know if it was the wind and the ocean, or the poster of a little green man in the pub at Westport where we stopped for more Guinness and Kilkenny, but that night I dreamt of a leprechaun.

Back home in Geneva, where we were then living, I started to write about a leprechaun called Ben. Ben wasn't green, though; he wore black velvet knickerbockers and a floppy white blouse. He had chin-length hair the colour of corn and would swing on my kitchen curtain rail by his knees. And he would tell me stories which I wrote down.

He told me about how he'd been to Japan, the old Japan of Anjin-San. Then he told me about the sushi trains in Tokyo and with great glee jumped into the bowl of jelly I was preparing. Boy, did he make a mess. He left me, saying he had to catch an electric storm to the land of the long white cloud, but that he'd be back.

I sent the story to a small magazine in Hiroshima and it was accepted. They were looking for a bit of whimsy and Ben must have jumped through their window just at the right moment. It was my first story in print.

There followed more stories about Ben riding rainbows and jumping into tales of far-off lands, and soon I had a full twenty pages which I entitled 'An Imaginary Friend'. It was the story of Liana and Ben. Ben kept having to go away to search for those infamous pots of gold. He would ride electric storms and rainbows, never tiring, never getting old. But Liana got old, as we all do, and her knees started aching. One day, Ben came back from one of his trips with a little bag of golden dust. He told Liana that the dust would ease the pain and that she should rub it into her knees. And as she did so, Liana began to shrink until she was the same size as Ben. He took her hand gently and guided her up a fresh new rainbow with an indigo bannister. They went slowly at first, for it was all uphill, but they eventually got to the top where they sat holding hands and dangling their legs until they faded away with the rainbow.

'An Imaginary Friend', the twenty-page story, was published in print by a magazine in America. I imagined it becoming an internet project that would teach children about stories and places all over the world. Maybe it still will. I sometimes wonder if I would have met Ben had I not been to Ireland to see Heinrich Böll's cottage, or snuggled up with James Joyce at a hearth near Belmullet. Or maybe it was just the leprechaun poster, or the Guinness and Kilkenny in the pub at Westport.

A Dublin Sunday

Elizabeth Brickley, Dublin

After Mass, we started the roast, usually beef. Mammy would don her fresh apron and I would be given the apples to peel and core for the apple tart. They were usually windfalls or bruised ones that the local grocer, Mr Byrne, would give to Mammy. We lived in a cottage in Phibsboro in Dublin, thirty minutes' walk from Nelson's Pillar. We had a kitchen, three bedrooms and an outside toilet. I was the youngest of five children and I never left my mother alone for a second, always hanging out of her as she cooked.

When the aroma of roast beef and apple pie began to fill the kitchen, my brothers emerged from the boys' room – young Teddy boys. When I was seven, and still small enough for him to lift, I was my brother Tom's jiving partner. Once Bill Haley was on the radio, Tom would pick me up and swing me over his head and under his legs and spin me around, while my other brother, Richard, was polishing his shoes and getting his saxophone from under the bed to play in St Thomas's Brass Band. God love him, I would collapse with laughter as soon as I saw him in the uniform. He was like a little Russian general.

Then all of a sudden, silence. Mammy and I exchanged glances. The family next door, having a row as usual. A good one, too – plenty of effing and blinding, words that meant nothing to me. The youngest boy, who was my age, would emerge from the house wearing a red surplice to go and serve Mass. He was closely followed by his mother, Mrs Moran, with her teeth clenched and her eyes raised to heaven. She would look into our kitchen window without a word and catch my mother's eye, as if to say, 'Mission accomplished. He's wearing it.'

The next person to pass the window was Johnny. An ageless man – in retrospect, I would guess he was fifty or sixty – he was homeless and squatted in one of the five cottages. I worried that he would die in a house fire, as he set his chimney on fire every Saturday night by placing an entire bag of coal in the grate, setting it alight, then forgetting about it and falling asleep. We were on first-name terms with at least three of the firemen.

The pubs would close from two until five and, as the cottages were located by the back entrance to our local, Daddy would push the door open at five minutes past two, and Johnny would push open his door at six minutes past. Mammy would lay Johnny's dinner on a tray, covered with a cloth to keep it warm – his roast beef and potatoes, his apple pie and custard. I would deliver it, listening to Johnny rooting in the darkness for sixpence, which would get me into the cinema that afternoon. I often wondered what lay behind the door, with its pungent smell of fire and water. I had only seen the inside once, when I noticed that he slept with his head on a pack of dough from the local bakery. I told Mammy not to bother sewing the flour sacks together to make Johnny a pillowcase, and Tom laughed and said that at least Johnny woke up to fresh bread every morning.

My job done, I would take off at high speed to the Boh (Bohemian) cinema, the centre of the world for every child in Phibsboro. My favourite film was *Some Like It Hot*. I would sit in the dark, blinking up at the screen and forgetting all about Johnny's big purple nose and singed eyebrows. Looking back, I suppose I was a fair-weather friend – but then, nobody's perfect!

Golden Goose Bay

Clare O'Beara, Dublin

I met Donal while on a weekend break in Galway. The weather had been kind but an autumnal chill drove me to seek the homely warmth of my hotel's turf fire in the evening. Donal, a strongly-built, middle-aged man, well-dressed with receding brown hair, came to spread his hands to the flames and soon we were enjoying a contemplative Guinness together.

'Beautiful country over here,' I remarked, having detailed my visit to Yeats's home, Thoor Ballylea, that day. 'But I should think it gets very bleak in winter.'

'Winter!' Donal chuckled and shook his head. 'The smell of turf smoke and the craic, they're the only good things about winter. Nothing much has changed here since I was a lad.'

After gentle encouragement he expanded on the subject.

'My father farmed in Mayo,' he told me, 'as they call it, "Mayo, God help us". There was the usual half-dozen of us children, running barefoot when we hadn't shoes and saving them for Sundays and school when we had. A trip to Westport would be a big occasion. I helped on the land and built more stone walls than I care to remember. I drove the milk to the creamery in the cart and dug potatoes and cut turf. Dad used to pay me a couple of shillings a week and I hated to take the money as he could barely support the family. One year I decided I'd had enough and I set sail for America.'

'Emigrated?' I nodded wisely. 'Hope you didn't expect the streets to be paved with gold.'

'Well,' he said, shrugging, 'they certainly weren't. There was no work there either. All I could come up with was to join the army. A Limerick lad I'd met signed up and instantly got posted to Korea. I never saw him again.'

'Was he killed?' I asked sympathetically.

'I don't know. I just never saw him again. Well, I asked around as to what was wise, because I didn't fancy Korea. And I got some very good advice.'

Donal paused to draw from his pint. 'I went up to Canada,' he continued. 'And signed up with the army there. They sent me to Labrador, to Goose Bay.'

I nodded. 'The Air Force base.'

'At the time they were establishing the early warning and atomic installations and I was detailed to guard duty.'

'Doesn't sound very exciting.'

'Didn't have to be,' he grinned. 'The pay was compensation. We were paid monthly and my first month's pay nearly made me weep. It would have bought my father's entire farm. I saved most of what I earned over the years.'

'Well done.' I knew plenty of emigrants whose unexpected riches had burnt holes in their pockets.

'I knew the value of money, for one thing, and for another, I found very little opportunity to spend. Goose Bay was a backward town of a few hundred souls, stuck on the south-west end of Lake Melville, over a hundred miles from the Atlantic. The Royal Canadian Air Force shared the base with their tenants, the US Air Force, and that was the only notable feature of life for miles around. I could never take to their light beer and I didn't marry there, so I accumulated my money, enough to come back here several years later, see my family was all right and set myself up here in Galway.'

'Good day for all of us when you did that, Mr Donal,' acknowledged the cheery voice of the barman. 'Sure you give us all work here and run a grand hotel for the tourists too.'

'Ah now, we don't do too badly.'

'But what you had to endure to get that money,' I marvelled. 'The cold, the snow, the isolation of Labrador…'

'Beautiful, though,' he assured me. 'And that's just the point I was making…Goose Bay was no hardship at all to me after winters in Mayo, God help us.'

Firedance

Barry Devlin, Ardboe, County Tyrone

In the 1970s Horslips toured widely across Ireland, England, Europe and the USA. It was a lot of fun. Our clothes and our stage sets were...em...pretty outrageous, actually. As well as fur-trimmed singlets and flares we had at one point in our career a stage show that featured two dragons sitting one on each side of Eamon Carr's bright-green drum kit.

These dragons were made of fibreglass and like everything else Horslippian – including my deeply tasteful shamrock bass – were designed by Charles O'Connor our fiddle/mandolin/concertina player and all-round centre of excellence.

These were no ordinary dragons.

For one thing they were 3-D replicas of mythical beasts from *The Book Of Kells* and were more like pug dogs than the dragons of children's books and animated films of the present day.

For another, they breathed fire during the song 'Sword Of Light'. To do this spectacular belching, they had metal-lined jaws with flash pans inside them. At the appointed time, Peter Clark, our lights man, would throw a switch and flash powder in the flash pans would go off.

Whoooosh! Just like that.

Usually it worked.

One night in England, though, in Colston Hall in Bristol, it spectacularly didn't. The flash went off OK but Peter had put too much powder in the trays and flaming particles sprayed on to the stage. To compound things, the jaws of one dragon caught fire. Melting fibre-glass dripped on to the boards.

We resolutely kept playing.

Peter looked around for the fire extinguisher, found none and seized the moment instead. He ran on stage and began stamping out the myriad little fires that had spread across the stage in front of the kit.

But here's the thing. Peter was a bit of a hippy and he was wearing clogs. Clogs with rubber tacked on to their soles.

It was the work of a moment for them, too, to catch fire.

Long hair flying, arms spread wide, Peter leaped around the stage like a beclogged Nureyev clothed in a gauzy veil of fire and smoke. Eat your heart out, Michael Flatley.

The music never missed a beat but the band members momentarily disappeared from view as we stepped into the shadows to hide from the baying crowd the fact that we were doubled up with laughter.

On our next tour there were mutterings in Bristol; 'Good gig, man. We really miss the firedancer, all the same.'

Summer Mania

Mary Mullen, Alaska (now living in Galway)

You eat outside with the neighbours, rush to soccer practice, take the bus to town just to hear the buskers on Shop Street and mow the lawn late at night. You entertain company and take a boat trip from Doolin to view the Cliffs of Moher with another set of visitors. You sleep late and don't worry about it because it is summer and you both deserve some lazy mornings. You try to keep the house somewhat presentable in case someone calls in for a cuppa and then you give up on that mission because the weather woman says there will be 'unsettled weather' starting tomorrow morning, so you say to your daughter, okay, put your shoes on, quick, we are going to take a hike. Now. Hurry.

'Naw, I don't feel like it. I want to watch *The Secret Garden*.'

And you say, come on, I'll *Secret Garden* you, which gets a quick smile from her and furthermore – being ever-vigilant about her safety – you throw in: we don't believe in secrets in this house, we have only surprises, remember? I'm surprising you by saying, get in the car, it's going to rain tomorrow, let's make hay while the sun shines. Her Down Syndrome makes idioms hard for her to decipher but she gets the point: there she is all cosy in the sitting room and now her wild-woman Mom is barking at her – hurry, into the car, we must have more summer fun. And finally, after running back into the house to get the mobile phone and a towel in case we jump into the sea, oh, and feed the cat – where is that cat? – you are off to somewhere beautiful.

You end up past Carron in County Clare. You hike up and

downhill and find yourselves at an amazing ring-fort with a 360-degree view of hills that kindly roll into one another. There are small purple flowers. You wish you knew their scientific name. The wind blows your daughter's hair away from her face, gives a quick snapshot of what she'll look like when she is thirty. Her gorgeousness gives you energy.

You hold hands, walking over the mossy rocks that could snap an ankle. Then you slow down, inhale the hand-holding moment, and realize that you haven't held hands since she was quite little. It feels so sweet, her eleven-year-old hand in yours. It is a lovely hand: her fingers are long and thin, her fingernails are tidily bitten short. The warmth of her hand radiates into the Burren.

You suggest running up the next hill. She flies up like a fairy, you huff and puff, your run turns to a walk half-way up. She yells, 'Come on, Mom, almost there!' You reach her at the pinnacle. You both automatically tumble into the grass and lie on your backs with your knees up. There is heat in the sun and in your hearts. You just lie there, holding hands and looking up at the clouds, catching your breath. She imagines what the clouds might say to each other: 'Hey dude, wanna dance? Naw, I'm on my way to the shop, gotta hurry, it's gonna rain mañana. Is that Polish, Mom, mañana?' No, you say, mañana is Spanish, and it definitely means tomorrow, good girl yourself.

Back in the car, she puts on music that you don't think suits the day, but you say nothing. Then you swing down to the Flaggy Shore. The tide is high. You run towards the sea while rolling up your jeans and you splash in and out and jump over the tangy surf. A blonde Labrador shakes water all over you. It feels good. You walk a few metres up the sand, lean your back against an ancient stone wall and lift your face up to the sun while she finds fascinating beach things.

Locals come all togged out for swimming. They smile at

you and your daughter and comment that the water is warmer today than yesterday. Crocosmias flutter orange along the road home. Posters in Kinvara advertise Cruinniú na mBád. Summer becomes autumn. You are glad that you got a bit manic about it while you could.

Surgical Wonderland

Deirdre Brennan, Waterford

Friday the eighteenth
The squeak of the door disturbed my sleep. I'd been moved into the private room that morning and was enjoying the silence after the madness of the six-bed public ward that had been my home since the previous Sunday. For the previous few hours, I hadn't been asked to help anyone to fasten their bra strap or get their mobile phone from under the bed or find the elusive television remote. I wondered if the others on the ward realised that I had had surgery too. Just because the surgical approach involved going through my nose as opposed to splitting my head open, it didn't make it any less brain surgery. The fact that they hadn't had to cut off 'my lovely long red hair' was a comfort to all the old dears on the ward. They had discussed it at length while I was in theatre.

I shifted in the bed and sat myself up, while trying discreetly to hide my feet underneath the dressing gown that was laid across the bed. My plan was fatally flawed as I had been using the same dressing gown to hide my vast collection of celebrity gossip magazines. Time spent in hospital is not kind to a girl's feet so I had a split-second decision to make. Did I want them to think I am obsessed with minor celebrities or someone with hooves? Then the memory of my reflection in the mirror that morning came back to me: two black eyes, a nose three times its normal size, nostrils that you could have driven a large armoured truck through, a face that was turning from black to blue to green with bruising, two swollen hands and puncture wounds from the daily blood tests all the way up to my elbows. I opted for covering the magazines. My looks were a lost cause but I just might be able to maintain the illusion of intelligence.

The consultant eased himself on to the bedside chair. He shook my hand gently, smiled and sighed. 'Ah, Miss Brennan, you are proving an interesting case.' My heart sank. I'd been in this hospital for five days and was beginning to understand the intricacies of doctor-speak. Being an interesting case was not a good thing.

Sunday the thirteenth
The bright torchlight stung my eyes. It had come from out of nowhere. And then the questions started.

'Where are you?'

That threw me even more than the beam that was scorching my pupils.

'Sorry. Excuse me?'

'Where are you?'

My confusion was interpreted as a hearing issue so the volume of the repeated question was considerably louder. My puzzlement had now changed into concern for this person. If she didn't know where we were, I was in serious trouble. She tapped the pen lightly and quickly on the edge of the folder she was holding.

'Dublin?' I suggested sheepishly.

Loud sigh. More tapping. 'Yes. Yes. But where?'

She had pocketed the torch and was scribbling efficiently into the folder. My eyes readjusted and spots of colour danced in the darkness in front of me.

'The northside? Beaumont Hospital? The neurosurgical ward?'

Big tick in the folder.

'Do you know what day it is? What is the date? Who is the Taoiseach?'

Aha, the 'is your brain still working' questions!

More ticks on the sheet. 'I'll be in to check on you during the night. Get some sleep and the surgical team will see you in the morning.'

With a brisk flick of the wrists, she was on the other side of the curtains. They swished back into place and I was alone on the bed, my legs dangling over the side. The ward was dark, apart from the single lamp that shone over my stack of pillows. Through the wall of windows on my left I could see faint blurred illuminations of Dublin. Blinking lights of planes landing at the airport flashed in the night sky. It seemed so peaceful out there. I was meditating on this strange tranquillity when the disgruntled snoring of the patient in the bed next to me brought me back to my new reality. Sounds of oxygen pumps and faint groans came through from the other side of the curtains. I eyed up the hospital ID bracelet that was my ticket into this Wonderland. I had fallen down the rabbit hole and it was time to walk through the door just as Alice had done.

Tuesday the fifteenth

The voice was gentle but insistent. 'Can you open your eyes for me, love?' Deep breath in. OK, I was alive. The blanket was scratchy and I felt hot, constrained and sweaty. My head was sunk into the pillow and each passing second brought an awareness of the 'discomfort' or 'pressure' that the doctors had alluded to before the surgery. Another lesson in doctor-speak. You can dress it up anyway you like but pain is pain and I hoped that the high-strength pharmaceuticals would be dished out soon. I thought that the best course of action was to approach this like a bad hangover. Keep as still and horizontal as possible, keep the eyes closed, have a snooze and when you do eventually wake up, you'll have slept through the worst of it and feel a hell of a lot better.

But the voice continued to ask. Kind. Soft. Gentle. Persuasive. Nonstop.

Gingerly I chanced it. Big mistake. The harsh glare of the fluorescent bulbs of the post-surgery ward assaulted my eyes. I was reminded of the ugly lights that come at the end of the disco to signal that it is definitely time to go home. My fluttering eyelids pleased the voice and it went to mark off some boxes on a checklist. 'Good girl, Deirdre. We'll have you back on the ward soon.'

Consciousness was proving an enemy of my sleeping plan. The blanket was still itchy and I wanted to ask the nurse if she could move it down a bit. But then I realised that underneath the blanket I was wearing a hospital gown that leaves little to the imagination and a pair of thigh-high support stockings. I stopped wriggling. The blanket could stay.

Wednesday the sixteenth
The hospital ward had a rhythm all of its own. The days were carefully divided into sections, each section separated by the rattle of the food trolleys. Breakfast, blood tests, tea, ward rounds and X-rays, lunch, nap time, consultant rounds, supper, visiting hours, tea, lights-out. Resistance to the routine was futile. You see the newbie admissions struggling against it, trying to assert their individuality in the midst of it, heading to the shop mid-morning, making phone calls in the afternoon. Madness.

'Are you all right there, Deirdre?'

'Yes, Maeve. Thanks.'

'Everything working all right? Everything moving?'

'Like clockwork, Maeve. Like clockwork.'

I made my way back to my bed from the bathroom. Toilet report filed with Maeve of Bed 32, I climbed under the blanket.

Another twenty minutes and the tea would be here. Dignity and privacy were long-abandoned concepts. Knowing my bathroom workings was important to Maeve and who was I to argue?

Thursday the seventeenth
Gaggle was the most appropriate word, I felt – a gaggle of junior doctors. Like geese. With their white coats, shiny stethoscopes and their standoffish manner, they appeared to be a distinct species. They gathered at the end of the bed, frowning, glancing at me briefly, then reviewing my notes.

'The nasal leak is more than we'd expect or like to see forty-eight hours post surgery.'

'Has she experienced any nausea, dizziness, metallic tastes in her mouth?'

'No. But the nasal packs are still in place and the leaking isn't improving.'

'Let's test for cerebrospinal fluid and leave the packs in for another twelve hours.'

One of the gaggle left the pack and approached me. He appeared hassled and addressed me while still studying my chart. 'Miss Brennan, how are you feeling?' His gaze didn't rise from the notes.

I dabbed the steady stream of fluid that was emanating from my nose. I took a deep breath and it bubbled at the back of my throat, so when I did manage to reply that I was doing OK, I sounded like a strangled frog. The head goose proceeded to ask me the same questions that the gaggle had just answered.

'Any nausea? Any dizziness? Metallic taste in your mouth?' He's still stuck to my notes.

No. No. No. Deep breath in. 'Look docs, I feel OK, apart from the obvious. I just think the fluid is normal nose juice as opposed to brain juice.'

This elicited a reaction. Slowly he looked up from the notes.

A smile slowly formed across his face. In a bemused voice, he asked what colour exactly I thought brain juice was.

Damn. I hadn't really thought my theory through so I said the first thing that came into my head. 'Green. Like kryptonite.'

The gaggle suddenly all became very interested in their shoes. My credibility was shot. With my searing insight into brain juice, I'd blown it. To them, I was always going to be just another clueless patient.

Friday the eighteenth

The consultant fingered the piece of paper thoughtfully and directed a kindly gaze at me.

'We've got the initial pathology back and the tumour presentation is more complicated then we'd expected,' My lips started to quiver and the supporting cast of SHO, registrar and intern looked on nervously, anticipating an emotional outpouring.

'As you know, Cushing's Disease is extremely rare. It affects five in a million. But this presentation of hyperplasic cells is a rare subset of affected patients...'

The quivering continued. I should have been paying more attention to what the consultant was saying.

'Further surgery...long-term management plan...craniotomy...hormone replacement therapy indefinitely...'

I was getting a long-term relationship with a doctor. It just wasn't exactly in the circumstances I had hoped for.

Despite my best efforts, a smile spread across my face. More adventures in Wonderland lay ahead.

'Doc,' I interrupted. 'I think we need to reassess my situation. I think we need to start using the term "very interesting case" to describe me.'

Higher, Stronger, Faster

Neville Cox, Ashford, County Wicklow

Johnny Giles, one of the great TV pundits in the game of football, once suggested that the biggest threat to the future success of the Irish soccer team was the fact that young people had overly easy access to Sony Walkmans. His logic was twofold. First, in order to be genuinely dedicated to any craft, football or anything else, one needs single-mindedness and kids cannot be completely committed to honing their soccer skills if their attention is distracted by whatever music is coming through the headphones. Secondly, the game of football cries out to its players for determination, courage and a never-say-die attitude, and these qualities cannot be achieved by people who easily obtain whatever they want without having to fight for it. What Giles said was reflective of the more broadly-expressed concern that the modern and highly pampered professional footballer who seems to be obsessed with how often and how publicly he can cheat on his wife and with how much money he can earn every week is sounding the death-knell for the beautiful game.

Despite the gloomy prognosis, there is, I am glad to say, good news for those who fear that the very future of football is at stake. Redemption and rebirth are at hand. For if you go to Wicklow town on any Tuesday evening you will see genuine warriors, with a gene pool directly inherited from Cúchulainn or Ron 'Chopper' Harris, who are prepared to die (or indeed kill) in order to force a small leather circular object into a net (which, like many of the players, has seen better days). They put their bodies on the line, for the glory of...well, in truth, there is no discernible glory, just the momentary feeling of having risen briefly to the level of a boyhood ambition to score a winning goal in a cup final, or lift the World Cup for Ireland. These are real players – not the modern celebrity types – who won't allow a groin strain or a wedding anniversary to prevent their participation. These are sportsmen.

If you don't believe me, cast a discerning glance over the group of players that gathers in Wicklow on a Tuesday. Look at them as they enter into their very own theatre of dreams with a glint in their eyes and an optimistic feeling that perhaps, just perhaps, this will be the night on which they don't score an embarrassing own-goal or commit some resounding faux pas which will stay with them long after the match is over. These are teachers (loads of teachers), actors, lawyers, computer technicians, bankers, insurance agents, social workers, barmen and others. Watch them as for one brief hour they shake off their normal persona and put on the clothes and the aura of world-class athletes.

Roy Keane would be proud of their ability to shout out orders at other teammates (if slightly less proud of their reluctance to obey the same orders themselves). Alex Ferguson would feel undermined by the constant will to win exhibited by our heroes. Sonia O'Sullivan would look wonderingly at the level of fitness on offer, especially in the opening three minutes of the game. Giovanni Trappatoni, listening to the often incomprehensible rhetoric they come out with (admittedly the product of vocal chords connected to overly-rapid pulse rates) would congratulate himself on the giant strides which he has made in competency in the English language. And members of the medical profession, surveying the weekly catalogue of injured knees, pulled calf muscles and severely bruised testicles, would clasp one another's hands in joy, aware that however drastic the recession, their services will always be needed.

But that's not all. It is true that the combat in the arena on a Tuesday evening is gladiatorial, but Desmond Tutu or Nelson Mandela would be proud of the spirit of peace and reconciliation that wafts through the adjoining carpark, like fog from the breaths of the exhausted players. No recrimination, no vendettas, no sex scandals (I think). Indeed no one can really remember the final score. And of course, no money changes hands.

This is the truly astonishing point. Unbelievably, no one has been paid a penny for the massive amount of energy that has been expended and the massive amount of commitment displayed over the preceding sixty minutes – even though, for some of us, such energy and commitment may exceed what we contributed in our place of work that day. Instead we, the players, pay for the privilege of running our middle-aged backsides into the ground.

This, I think, is real sport; certainly it is much more real than the glorified and increasingly badly-acted reality television programme that is professional soccer. There is determination – but our game is entirely about competing and not about winning. There is a huge reward for playing but it is measured in good health, friendship and positive endorphins rather than in money. There are no adoring and compliant female fans, but for thirteen men, none of whom are native to Wicklow, it has been a means of meeting people within the community. Joy, good health, enthusiasm, determination and playing the game for the sake of playing – these are the true Corinthian values that made sport great, before inflated wages, sponsorship deals, TV broadcasting contracts and all the other trappings of professionalism turned the game of football into just any other business run by remarkably typical businessmen.

And that is why the game of football on an increasingly dilapidated astro-turf pitch in Wicklow on a Tuesday night is so special. It is a shining example of that most excellent of things: a pursuit which has nothing but positive connotations for all who take part in it and with no accompanying corporate bullshit.

Our bodies may be aging, our first touch may not be what it once was and our replica shirts may be a couple of years out of date, but in our hearts we are still eighteen, and still playing, like Roy of the Rovers, for a team which is competing for the highest possible stakes and for whom our involvement is indispensable.

First Love

Thady Dunne, Dublin

Eleanor came from Dublin to spend a few weeks with her cousins in a small town in County Tipperary. She was unlike any of the local girls: an exotic creature, a vision, highly washed, sparkling clean, dressed in bright clothes and white shoes. Even her name was exotic as local girls had mundane names like Mary, Bridget and Anne. And, of course, she was amazingly pretty!

She was about our age but years ahead in sophistication and my friends and I watched her from afar, all too shy and inexperienced to approach her. What would you say?

However, I thought it likely that I could be the chosen one, if I could figure out how to go about it.

You know the saying, 'You can't be too thin or too rich.'

Well, part of that applied to me and it wasn't because I had any money.

Still, with my hair plastered with Brylcreem (it was the custom of the day but you needed to have an older brother for the supply) and wearing round, wire-rimmed spectacles long before John Lennon made them fashionable, I cut, I thought, a somewhat dashing figure.

I wasn't into GAA: I was more a warrior type, skilled in the construction and use of bows and arrows, swords and spears from raw materials provided gratis by the local forestry.

We knew little (make that nothing) about the matter of male-female interaction. Our reading material – Biggles, the Famous Five and the Secret Seven – yielded no clues. Nor did

First Love

the education system, provided by the clergy and the Christian Brothers. The Brothers taught us many things – Maths, Latin, Chemistry – all through the medium of Irish. Nothing, however, through either medium, about biology, anatomy or relationships. This was rural, Catholic Ireland in the 1950s. Brothers didn't deal in sex: not that they let on to us anyway!

But if you studied them carefully there was possibly information to be gleaned from the unlikely source of the William books by Richmal Crompton.

William's sister, named Ethel, if I recall correctly, sometimes got involved in affairs of the heart, and was assisted, unasked and usually with unexpected results, by William.

I can't remember exact details but one scenario involved rescuing the loved one from a burning building, which was bound to impress her no end.

I couldn't recall ever seeing a burning building in the town and setting fire to the house where Eleanor lived didn't seem such a great idea, especially as she was staying in the home of a local Garda sergeant. I knew instinctively he just wouldn't understand. So that was no help.

Another possibility was saving her from a runaway horse but the few horses that were around just seemed to plod about in a bored manner, stopping from time to time to provide welcome compost for rose bushes, so that wasn't a runner.

My dilemma remained unresolved until the miracle happened one day.

I was out in the back yard and had just constructed a new bow. I was testing it with some of my best arrows, when the back door opened and my mother ushered out the *vision*!

She had come for me at last. I knew that she must have been hugely impressed, but she managed to conceal it well. She had been sent to me on a mission by her cousins, who had written from the Gaeltacht. They were in urgent need of comics, preferably glossy Dell ones, and had targeted me, a well-known comic-dealer, as the likely source.

Here was my big chance. So what did I do?

I'd like to be able to say that I quietly charmed her with my personality and impressed her with my rural skills.

The fact was, of course, that I blew it completely, mumbling that I was sorry, I didn't have any comics that they hadn't already seen.

She left and I went back to my work, thinking of what might have been, not that I really had much idea of what that might be.

Soon afterwards she returned to the city, leaving behind at least one broken heart.

But, fortunately, a ten-year-old broken heart heals quickly, I got over it and soon my fickle attentions (focused, certainly, but only vaguely understood) switched to another lovely – Anne, a gorgeous and aloof blonde princess, daughter of the bank manager.

Epiphany

Liz Quinn-Einstein, Wicklow

Vivienne had very set ideas about religion, in particular the Catholic Church. She had spent a childhood in Ireland being drilled in catechism and all the other 'isms' that went with her parents' very devout views on the subject. Having married an atheist with a Jewish background she was determined on her return to the land of her birth that her only child was never going to endure the mindless devotion expected of her as a youngster. Erika had been christened as a gesture of goodwill towards her parents, although not in a Roman Catholic Church but a Marionite one, and in Aramaic, not English.

Having looked around the area she lived in, Vivienne was disappointed to find that non-denominational primary schools were not available either in that area or anywhere else in the land of saints and scholars. She therefore settled on the next nearest option, that of an inter-denominational co-educational Irish school. She had reservations about the 'Irish' bit but knew her daughter was very bright and consoled herself with the thought that any language learnt in a colloquial way would encourage an ear for more widely-spoken languages.

From when Erika started junior infants, Vivienne secretly dreaded the day that Holy Communion would become an issue. By the time Erika had reached second class she was aware that although the school claimed 'inter-denominational' status, in real terms 95 per cent of her daughter's peers were from Catholic homes. They had discussed the alternatives with Erika and she was in complete agreement with them on transubstantiation. Holy Communion was not going to happen in their household, that was non-negotiable. It was therefore decided that Erika would take part in the religious instruction classes so that she did not feel alienated from her friends. Her father looked on with benign amusement when she came home with the age-old concepts of original sin and Adam and Eve. Even Vivienne smiled to herself as Erika discussed her various misdemeanours in terms of 'not loving enough', rather than committing sins.

Just after mid-term break in February a note arrived from school about First Confession. It was to be a school event at the local church and parents were welcome. With trepidation Vivienne agreed to go with Erika to support her friends. It was at least twenty years since she had been in a church, apart, of course, from the christening. She looked around with interest and watched as the other children and their parents prepared for the occasion. Erika's teacher seemed surprised and pleased when she saw the two of them. She knew that Vivienne had little idea of what to expect as she had consciously avoided all discussions on the affair and had voiced her views on more than one occasion. She explained that the children would confess their sins to the priest on the alter one by one, out of earshot of their parents and other prying adults but that sin was not a word used any more, Vivienne suggested 'character defects' as an option and was met with a giggle – no, that was not what transgressions were called these days. Sin had now become the act of 'not showing enough love'.

As the children settled down and the rhythm of the ceremony established itself, Vivienne began little by little to question her views. Gone were the rigidity and structure she had grown up with and abhorred. One by one, Erika's classmates went up to the altar and returned to their parents' pews with the glowing joy of innocence returned to their faces. She sneaked a look at her daughter as they watched her best friend Patsy return and was certain from her daughter's wistful look of wonder that she had made a mistake. She quickly asked her whether she had changed her mind and sensed her daughter's indecision, although her willingness to please her mother was touching.

Without saying a word, she took her by the hand and led her to the altar. Erika beamed her thanks to Vivienne throughout this very special Confession. She realised that by being so determined not to repeat the mistakes of her own parents, she had made a different set of mistakes. Zealots come in many guises. Her daughter was growing up and with that came choices, choices about how to live and what to believe. They were very personal and private choices, choices that could be made only by Erika. Vivienne finally understood that just as her parents had limited her choices, she was limiting her daughter's. With lightened hearts they left the church.

The Beerosphere

Cormac Eklof, Dublin

As I cycle through the Phoenix Park, the late-morning sun beating down on me, my phone rings from deep down in my pocket. I pull the bike up to answer. As I fish for my phone I notice a herd of peaceful-looking deer grazing in the field to my right. The other oddity that registers is that there isn't one single car driving past. Not one. Normally this would be a busy thoroughfare, particularly at this time of day on a weekday.

The 2002 World Cup showdown between underdog Ireland and enormous favourite Spain is about to kick off and I am still a good ten minutes from the bar where I have arranged to meet my friends. Because of the time difference between Ireland and Japan, the game is kicking off at roughly noon, Irish time.

The office was a complete sham earlier that morning. As a team-leader, I was resigned to missing the game but one by one my team called in with a variety of illnesses. As the phone calls built up in number, the illnesses became odder and odder as regards symptoms.

My personal favourite was the last standing member of my team of software engineers. 'I can't make it in today. I broke my nose on the lawn mower yesterday evening.'

My boss came by an hour before kick-off and simply shook her head disdainfully at the completely transparent status of her missing team. She relayed the news that this scene was repeating itself all over the city, and then, with a simple smile and shrug of her shoulders, she sent me off on a half-day. No point in a team leader being around with no team to lead. Not today, of all days.

On my way out the door I make a frantic call to my best friend Gordy. The crew is all meeting in a bar, an hour before kick-off, to make sure they get a spot. That is Gordy on the phone now, telling me to hurry up, the bar is already packed and the game about to kick off. 'Oh, and what are ya drinkin'?"

I pedal furiously out the Parkgate Street gates of the Phoenix Park. As I scream down the quays, I can see this busy thoroughfare all the way up towards the Ha'penny Bridge and the heart of the city. Only today there is no busyness, no hustle and very little bustle. Dublin's streets lie almost empty. A lone car trundles lazily down the quays and two pedestrians, old women, walk slowly towards the centre. That's it. Apart from that, it's a ghost town.

The road the pub is on is completely empty. There isn't one car or a single person in sight. It's extremely quiet, except for the din emanating from the bar itself, the noise getting louder as I approach. The pub is completely overrun with people. There are dozens of hopefuls, milling around outside, unable even to get in the front door. I spot a side door and sneak in.

In front of me is a heaving, colourful and transfixed crowd. The bar is jam-packed, so much so that movement inside is almost impossible. Worried faces are glued to the big screens; the match has already begun, Spain have taken the lead very early. Ireland is struggling. The World Cup dream is on thin ice.

I spot Gordy, his wife Sal and the rest of the crew; they have a small area amongst the throng with a great view of the main big screen. Gordy, a mighty man, has a huge paw wrapped around Sal, protecting her from the throng of people, and the other wrapped around a pint of Guinness. Inching my way over to them through the heaving mass of bodies, I am grabbed into the fold by Gordy. In a split second, I am brought up to speed. Spain looks too strong, Ireland looks too nervous. Oh, by the way, here's your pint. Thanks man, good health.

The match ebbs and flows, pulsates back and forth. At half time, it is almost as if the entire crowd of hundreds exhales for the first time. The half-time whistle is greeted by a well-lubricated, audible sigh and the swell of the crowd moves towards and then away from the bar as refuelling occurs in the break.

Ireland emerges for the second half with rekindled passion and heart. Irish manager McCarthy brings on the veteran Niall Quinn, who quickly unsettles the Spanish defence with his size. The excitement builds. The crowd is throbbing at this stage. There is a beating pulse and every moment of note is greeted with roars, moans and curses, directed at teams and referee alike.

The brilliant imp Damien Duff glides into the Spanish area and is chopped down. Penalty! A moment of stunned silence follows the collective intake of breath as Ian Harte steps up to take it. Cruelly, he misses, shoulders slumped and breath exhaled in deflation. The match moves close to a finish.

Wise heads nod. We had a great run and the draw with Germany alone was worth it.

But fate and a glamorous Swedish referee intercede. With the clock showing eighty-nine drama-packed minutes, a Spanish defender tries to remove Niall Quinn's jersey as a free kick is taken. Anders Frisk, he of the flowing hair, Scandinavian tan and hyperbolic arm movements and facial expressions, dramatically points to the spot. This time the little assassin Robbie Keane steps up to take it. Stranger holds stranger. Mouths are open but no sounds emerges. The entire nation holds its breath.

He scores.

Chaos. The bar erupts. The ball of humanity assembled explodes in a single noise, a kind of a roar of relief and excitement. Those holding their pints – and they are very many – throw their arms in the air. For a split second the volume of beer thrown to the sky hangs like an ozone layer. Gravity ensures that it falls to earth, soaking the uncaring masses, who are still dancing and hugging and shouting. Gordy leans in, practically kissing my ear, 'Did you see that? All the beer in the air? It was like a Beerosphere!'

This is the finest moment in the 2002 Irish World Cup dream. Spain's class and talent comes to the fore in the eventual penalty shoot-out. They are through. Ireland are out, gallant Keane-less heroes. Everyone is drunk. Gordy and Sal are gone. The bar empties quickly, some fools going back to work, drunk; others just needing fresh air or food. As I follow the mass movement towards the exit, a bear of a man I have never met before catches my eye. We pause briefly, then hug, a massive, enveloping hug. 'Some feckin match, eh?'

Yep, some feckin' match all right.

Gift of Garrykennedy

Kevin Wells, Baltimore, MD, USA

I first told my uncle, Father Tommy, about Krista in a small pub near the Shannon. We were in of one of Ireland's charming harbour villages, Garrykennedy. It was one of those nights when I wished I could crush every clock in the house to lasso time. Tommy had rented a giant farmhouse in the tiny town of Portroe in County Tipperary and dispatched an invitation for family to visit him in the heart of Ireland. So fifteen of us or so gathered at the old house that was hedged in by the Shannon and endless, wavy acres of grassy farmland. Days that were filled with leisurely travel and promenades into the meadows were followed by evenings charged with storytelling – the kind that awakened the cows and would have made Yeats happy. For a three-day span at the end of the rental period, Tommy and I had the farmhouse to ourselves. And things got even better.

A one-lane road led from the farmhouse to the riverside village of Garrykennedy, which offered up two pubs like jackpot-winning lottery tickets. These candlelit places had magic within their walls – where part of the musical entertainment might be a white-haired widow easing from a mahogany bench to resurrect an emigration song in the old language. This was the authentic 'craic,' as Tommy would often say, where timeworn traditions unfolded with an intermingling of mystery and sacredness, like transubstantiation at Mass.

Since it was a comfortable evening, Tommy and I decided to walk past the smattering of houses that were far off the road down to Garrykennedy. We passed lines of hedgerows, fields choked with ruby-red corn poppies and meandering stone 'penny fences' that knifed through open bog lands and pastures. The summery hum of insects and grunts and groans of heifers and sheep followed us as we laughed and laughed about the events that had unfolded that week. Townsfolk, who passed by in tiny, slow-moving cars so as to not kick up dust, lifted index fingers briefly off their steering wheel, the old way of saying 'Good evening and God bless.'

We had worked up a thirst after our thirty-minute walk and the bartender was serving Guinness so he obliged us. We seemed to be trailing the locals in the pint count so we attempted to catch up at a table in the corner. There we could watch locals enter.

Tommy was immediately in his element. Ireland had his heart. And its people helped it to beat. He always said it was 'its people' that made Ireland the eternal emerald it is. This was the second occasion that I spent time with Tommy in Ireland. Like our earlier two-week trip to Ireland's western coast, I noted his silly transition to the brogue mere hours after his plane taxied him to the terminal. Ahh, hello dare, sir. Fer sure, you can join us for the Guinness. Honest, be a shame if ya din't.

'Tommy, I think I found a good one,' I told him.

'Tell me.'

'Well, her name's Krista and she's Italian and Irish and beautiful. She loves riding horses more than anything in the world. She's quiet. And she doesn't remind me of any of the others.'

'Keggy, that's probably a good thing.'

'Thanks, Father…What I mean to say is, that she has a good heart. That's what I know for sure. And that she loves me…she reminds me of Mom.'

'Really?'

'Well, she doesn't care about all the stuff out there, like Mom doesn't, you know. She keeps it simple and appreciates the important things. She loves children and loves God. You should see the way she works with the kids she's giving riding lessons to.'

'Sounds like the right one…Do you love her?'

'Yeah, I think so.'

'Well, then – if you think God has brought Krista to you – I couldn't be happier for you.'

I remember the Shannon breeze that flitted through the pub's open door that night and the Gaelic ballads dug from the souls of fishermen, farmers and old widows. I remember the way Tommy struck up conversations with humble-hearted locals whose sun-shot cheeks bore splotchy blue capillaries that rambled like Irish road maps. He inadvertently mentioned to some that he was a priest and suddenly the table spilled over with fresh pints.

As we walked back to the farmhouse beneath a blanket of twinkling starlight, the smoked-earth smell of peat hung in the Shannon air like Irish incense. And the night seemed like a benediction to the wholesomeness of old-country ways. Christ felt so close, as if he was tucked in with us between the rushes and hedgerows.

Tommy witnessed our marriage a little over a year later. 'I'll be there for you,' he told Krista at the end, 'throughout it all.'

Tommy was murdered by a homeless man high on crack cocaine three years ago. I have thought of his words many times since and still feel he is there with us.

An Irish Exile

Anne O'Curry, Foxrock, County Dublin

Soon after I left school in Dublin I packed my rucksack and flew Aer Lingus to Paris where I planned to improve my French and work as an au pair. The pace of this major European capital took me by surprise as it was very much faster than sleepy Dublin in the 1970s. But I very quickly adapted to the sounds of a new language and the delicious smells that came from living above a pâtisserie in the centre of the city.

My first job was working for a French family. Suffice it to say I did not stay too long as we did not agree on many things. I then went to work for an Irish family with three young children, so instead of sampling the best of French cuisine I was enjoying plates of Irish stew and salmon and spuds and coming home to the smell of freshly baked soda bread. Needless to say, any friend or relative who came to stay arrived with gifts of rashers, sausages and black puddings and woe betide anyone who forgot to pack Barry's tea in their suitcase.

In the late afternoon, when the children came home from school, friends regularly dropped in for a chat for a cup of tea. One such visitor was a journalist, an expat called Francis who had left Ireland in his twenties. He loved to hear news from Dublin. It became almost a ritual with him to drop in some time after four o'clock and then leave us at six to visit another Irish friend who lived close by. His routine never changed.

One day curiosity got the better of me and I asked him who his friend was. He casually replied, 'Sam.'

'Sam!' I echoed.

'Yes, he lives on his own. He is a bit of a recluse, really, but I've known him a long time. Actually he grew up in Foxrock in a house not far from your own in Dublin.'

'Sure, maybe I know him then or I might have heard of him.'

'Well most people have heard of him, but not many have met him.'

'And what is Sam's second name?' I asked.

But my question got lost in the conversation for some minutes as the children began to chase around the table, eventually knocking the milk jug to the floor. There it lay scattered in pieces while the Siamese cat contentedly lapping up the spilt milk.

'Sorry, Francis. Continue where you left off. We were talking about your friend.'

'Yes. You wanted to know his surname.'

'That's right!'

'It's Beckett,' he replied exactly as he might have done if it were Murphy or Donoghue.

I put the two names together and slowly pronounced them, 'Sam .. Beckett. Samuel . . . Beckett.'

'Yes, that's him,' Francis confirmed.

As someone who has always had an interest in the Irish theatre, I was taken by surprise.

'You really mean Beckett the playwright?' I asked.

'Yes. Yes, of course. You know he does not go out much as he is a bit of a recluse but I've known him for years and he likes me to visit.'

'I'd love to meet him.'

'Would ye now?'

'Yeah, I really would. Will you ask him will he see me?'

'Right so, ' replied Francis with a smile, as he stepped into the street, again checking his watch. He was aware that he was late and knew that Beckett would be waiting.

I counted the days until Wednesday came around again but Francis failed to appear. The following week I waited but again he did not come. Three weeks later he arrived with a smile, explaining that he had been on holidays but had forgotten to mention it.

I was not so interested in his holiday and much more interested in whether he had asked his friend whether he would see me.

'Oh yes, indeed. I asked Beckett if he'd see you but he sent his apologies to say he is not seeing anyone at present.'

Coming from a family with a strong background in the world of theatre it would have been a milestone in my life to have had even a cup of tea, never mind a glass of good French wine, in the company of the master of Irish theatre.

Things Disappear

Fred Johnston, Galway

My aunt believed that I should know where I was going to be buried. We would be in the kitchen, summery evening sun whacking through the window, I'd be washing my hair in the Belfast sink and thinking about the disco and she'd ask me if I knew where I was going to be buried. She was very serious about it. It was important to her and, moreover, it should have been important to me. I wasn't interested and was faintly amused. But she would raise her glass of bottled stout to her lips and ask me again. She'd emphasise the importance of it all. She'd name great graveyards in which all her brothers and sisters and her parents were buried. I could choose one of them. I expected her to produce a catalogue.

This obsession or concern with where I was to be buried seems, as I look back on it, to have its roots in a real fear about loss of identity and notions of oblivion. At the end, she seemed to be saying, there is only the closeness, the proximity, of one's own dead. There is nothing else. Perhaps not even God, who knows? God hadn't done much for her in any case. As I edged out the front door she would ask me to bless myself but there was never any water in the tiny plastic font nailed to the wall. When she died I knew nothing about it and to this day have no idea where she is buried. And, of course, she doesn't know either.

Things disappear. Graves disappear. The long black American Cadillacs that, somewhat absurdly, ferried my grandparents to a graveyard in Tallaght when Tallaght was truly the distant countryside, have disappeared too, with their smell of real leather and cheap perfume and cigarette smoke from uncles and aunts who alternately wept and argued. I felt like royalty in those cars, cruising up through Dublin with men stopping to doff their caps and women in headscarves making the Sign of the Cross: it was choreography, it was opera. Yet a dozen years ago I walked and walked through the sodden grass and up the water-oiled paths of that same ancient cemetery and there was no sign, no sign anywhere, of the headstone marking my grandparents' last resting place. Paths had been widened, greens restructured; I may have been walking over their old bones, for all I knew. Knowing that I had stood with my own weeping and solemn parents by a soggy hole somewhere in there was of no use. The grave was gone. No one on earth now knew where they had been buried.

On a country crossroads in Northern France, near a village that had a 'Rue des Juifs', which was now just a ploughed field, I found, neat and tidy and washed white, a square of tiny headstones, the inscriptions half in Arabic and half in French. Here, under French trees and scrupulous French skies, eight young men from a Moroccan regiment had given their lives for France, a country that meant little to them, in the face of a German tank attack. The details were all there, though there wasn't a soul or a vehicle or a house anywhere around. This is where these young men had their graves, or one might imagine so. In truth it was impossible to know where they were buried, or what of them was left to bury. They formed a geographic location, a small one at that, and little more. The carved crescent moons on the white headstones said something but not very loudly. Did any of them have aunts or grandmothers who, as these young men shaved and Brylcreemed themselves for a night out, asked them whether they knew where they'd be buried?

I think my aunt wanted me to know who I was, to attain, even at the end of my life, a rootedness I did not then possess.

The only property, the only piece of land I would ever own, she may have thought, or that I could at least lay claim to, would be that muddy, gloopy hole in some Irish field, and soon enough that too would vanish. But it was all anyone could wish for. It was also, perhaps, part of a desperate Irish need to have land, absurd as that may seem, manifesting itself in an equally absurd worship of acquiring property in the recent Celtic Tiger days. I am no sociologist.

Land seems to be the womb into which every Irish soul wishes to return. Men will murder for it, brother on brother, women will conspire for it, children will ruin themselves at law for it.

In the graveyard at Roquebrune, high on a cliff's edge overlooking the Mediterranean, the poet W.B. Yeats was laid to rest. Because land is so scare on the cliffside, one is not automatically interred in the one grave forever. I almost said 'for life'! A grave needs to be leased. Yeats's grave was leased only for one year due to a daft oversight and then the poor man's bones were dumped in the public ossuary nearby. All would have been well had not wishes been expressed to have him returned to Ireland. There followed a grotesque, Gothic scrambling in the ossuary by torchlight for his bones; there was talk of a pelvis with a truss. At any rate, some bones were transferred into the coffin that took him home, though we may never know whose. I have stood in the beauty of Roquebrune graveyard high above the bushes, the exotic flowers and the blue sea. One might wish to be buried there. But alas, there is a waiting-list.

A little of Yeats and presumably a little of some Roquebrune worthies was dutifully laid to rest under Ben Bulben. Of course, it is not done to mention this too loudly. We, not Yeats, have determined where his grave is. It is in Sligo and no one mentions Roquebrune or the South of France.

It would be comforting in an odd way to think that a whole

country might consider the location of one's grave to be of such national importance. Such was not the ambition of my aunt, for whom the thought of the loneliness of being buried somewhere other than with 'your own' was unbearable, and perhaps that was it in the end.

I think she was lonely in life: she who never travelled much had watched her family move away from her in one way or another. She could not have managed the dreadful truth that we may wish as much as we like but, in the end, other hands will direct us into the earth, foreign or otherwise. I hope someone knows the location of her grave. For her sake.

Mind Yourself

Fiona Deverell, County Laois (now living in Dún Laoghaire)

We had arrived in our family car, with my newly acquired, huge black suitcase in the boot – now finally packed after weeks of build-up, lists checked and double-checked. The suitcase had occupied the spare room at home for several weeks while the items on the List were assembled and added to it. My mother and grandmother had discussed and shopped and whirred at the sewing machine. Name tapes were ordered from Cash's, to be sewn on to each individual sock and shirt. My father had telephoned friends with daughters who might have had used uniform items, sports gear or books to sell or give away. I had come home from primary school every day to find a new addition to the pile. I had had several 'fittings' and even sessions of uniform-modelling for the neighbours, with my father taking photos while my two sisters looked on, envious of all the attention I was getting. Finally, the last item was ticked and the lid of the suitcase closed. My father had added a brown leather belt around its girth for extra security. He was the only member of the family who could lift it.

Inside were the strange new possessions required for life at boarding school – a drawstring bag for my hairbrush and comb; another for my shoe polish and brushes; another for laundry (my grandmother had made all these from floral curtain fabric). There was a Bible for personal use and a long list of clothing with a minimum number of shirts, jumpers, underwear, skirts. Some were new, most were second-hand, everything had required alteration, to be cut down and re-hemmed to suit my strangely small body. At almost twelve, I could still fit easily into clothes for an eight-year-old. My feet were size two. The hockey boots bought from a girl who had outgrown them were size four and a half, the smallest available, and my mother had resourcefully stuffed the toes with newspaper. I had been given a hockey stick almost as tall as myself. All these things were now mine, labelled with name tags and permanent marker. I had never experienced ownership of anything really, apart from my toys, and all those had been left behind in my bedroom at home. They weren't on the List.

It was a sunny day and there was a bustle of cars pulling in and out of the sweeping drive in front of the school's main residence. This was a large Victorian house, with two double-fronted storeys over a basement, set in several acres of grounds. The outside was pretty with flower beds full of roses and sloping lawns and terraces around the gravelled front. It looked like the set for an Agatha Christie novel: Miss Marple could have arrived at any moment. I felt I was holding my breath so that I could focus on this drama and its colourful cast. Everywhere there were girls, greeting one another, calling out to one another – to me it seemed they knew every other girl, every teacher. In a few corners younger girls shed tears and hugged their parents and siblings, while older ones held out their hands and haggled for extra five-pound notes from their fathers, or shot filthy looks towards their mothers, before gathering up their bags and hurrying inside.

We walked through this excitement, my father carrying the suitcase and my mother looking nervous. I watched it all as if it was a play on the stage. Quite quickly, I realised I was one of only a few girls wearing uniform. We had not known the dress code for today, and my mother, always cautious, had decided that full uniform would be advisable. Now my large grey jumper felt far too warm in the sunshine as I watched girls in jeans and T-shirts busily running in and out of the glass front doors. Someone should have turned down the sunshine: the summer ended yesterday, I thought.

In the large hallway inside, the noise was overwhelming – shouting, laughing, giggling, huddled earnest conversations. The hall smelt of lavender wax floor polish and fresh air – every door and window seemed to be open. The front hall had a tiled black-and-white floor; glass cabinets on either side displayed silver trophies and plates etched with names and dates. There was an old upright piano on which sat a large hand-bell. An elegant staircase with blue lino and white Victorian bannisters was alive with older girls, running up and down, grabbing one another's arms and asking, 'Have you seen so and so?'

I looked up to see high, bright landings and a glass dome in the centre of the top-floor ceiling, which shed light down through to where we stood. My parents spoke to the teacher on duty in the hallway, ticked my name on a list and enquired as to which was to be my dormitory. The teacher loomed above me in a tweed skirt and brown cardigan. She was wearing a green patterned silk scarf around her neck like the ones my mother sometimes wore on her head. For a moment she glanced down at me. She spoke to my mother: 'Turn left through that door, then left again, dormitory four,' she said.

We went through a deeply panelled door and on to a small landing with an entirely different atmosphere. It was dark and offered access up and down by a second, smaller and much less imposing set of stairs. Here there was dark-green lino and no natural light. A bare bulb struggled to show the way. The girls here passed up and down the stairs quickly and quietly. This was the staffroom landing. Maybe this would have been the servants' area or back stairs area of the original house. A door off this landing had the number four on it. It was a pleasant surprise to find that it opened into a large bright room at the front of the house, which must have been, at one time, for dancing in, or for banqueting. The lino in here was a shiny brown, and the high walls were painted white, so that the fine old plaster work and fireplace were shrouded out of significance. Now it had rows of pine bunk-beds, on which girls sat with parents, unpacking, whispering or silent. From outside we could hear the clamour of excitement as second to sixth years moved with ease into their dorms in familiar surroundings but in here, the air seemed heavy and tense. The hushed conversation and the smell of freshly laundered sheets made the room feel like a hospital ward. A group of four girls sat chatting quietly on a bed nearest the large bay window; they seemed to know one another. They glanced in our direction but the other girls, with their parents, did not seem to notice us. Each was intent, concentrating, holding her breath.

The beds were not made up. There was a pile at the end of each with two white sheets, two blankets and a pink candlewick bedspread. My mother made up the bed while my father hefted the suitcase on to a chair.

'Have you got your padlocks?' he asked.

I had five. They were on the List – one for my clothes-locker, one for my boot-locker, one for my tuck box, one for my book-locker in the prep hall and one for my book-locker near the classrooms. My father had selected five different brass padlocks from the local hardware providers and now he talked me carefully through the mechanism and key shapes. He had also made me a wooden tuck box to the size specified on the List and burned my initials into the lid with a hot poker. The box was stocked with homemade fruitcake and bars of chocolate. It was the one thing my father had taken on as his personal project, giving advice on what to bring and telling me cheerful stories about his own days at boarding school. He had maintained a cheery exterior all day, but he was tense – not in his usual position of captain on the bridge. Now he went to the row of tall, narrow lockers against one wall. They all stood with their doors open but each one appeared to have already been filled with clothes and toiletries. 'This one's empty,' he said, pulling open a larger one just inside the door.

'That's for the prefect,' came a voice from the little group at the end of the room.

I was suddenly aware that we had been noticed. Someone had been observing us and listening to our quiet conversation. An older girl, maybe a sister of a first year, repeated, 'That's for the prefect. She gets a bigger locker and that's her bed but she's not here yet.'

She pointed to the only single bed in the room, next to the bottom bunk which was now mine.

'All these lockers are taken. You'll have to go downstairs and use another one,' the girl said.

Now I woke up and reality bit hard. The others in the room, about ten girls and a few parents, were all looking at the three of us. Clearly we were the last to arrive, I had got the least desirable bed in the place, there were no lockers left and all the others knew one another. I felt suddenly tiny and inadequate and utterly inferior. When I turned towards my parents they were looking unsure and out of their depth. The older girl turned back to her conversation. She had not offered to show us where to go. We hesitated. She sighed deeply, got off the bed she had been sitting on, and in a bored tone said, 'I'll show you.'

She led us out of the room, into the dark stairwell and down two flights to a stone-floored basement. This part of the house was entirely different: there were no windows to the outside, and the light came from bare yellow bulbs. There was a musty smell mixed with a faint odour of oil from the boiler in the next room.

'Feels damp down here,' my father said, putting his hand against the wall.

'It's fine. I'm sure they wouldn't have lockers down here if it was damp,' said my mother in a breezily cheerful tone.

Under the stairs were four lockers adrift without a dormitory. Only one was unfilled. My father quickly hung a padlock on it to 'bag' it. We began to carry my new belongings down to the basement locker in batches, stowing everything in the cubby holes and on the shelves inside. Another girl directed us to the boot room, also in the basement, where I located my boot-locker and stored my hockey stick and boots, my tennis racquet and runners and the drawstring bag containing my shoe polish and brush, all as directed by the List, which my mother had been carrying with her since our arrival. My father supervised the padlocks and made me lock and unlock each one several times until he was satisfied I would have no difficulty.

My tuck box was placed on a shelf in a cupboard in the tuck room, and when we found the prep hall, I found a sticker with my name on it on book-locker Number 19. Thankfully, it was in the second tier and not too high for me to reach. Also in the prep pall were stacks of folding wooden desks. The number 19 was etched on a brass plate on a light-coloured desk. This and its corresponding locker was to be mine from First Year to Fourth Year, to be used during supervised study in the evenings. The List had called for a small piece of fine sandpaper, a tin of wax polish and a polishing cloth to be stored in the book-locker. This was for the maintenance of the desk during my four-year stewardship. I can still picture the golden colour of the wood and its individual knots and whorls. Every term for four years I found it again from its markings, like a puppy in a litter. If the desk still exists, I am sure that to this day, I could walk into a room and pick it out by sight from among all the others.

When all had finally been unpacked my giant black suitcase was to be placed with the others in the front hall. At some point, they were removed by unseen hands and stored in the trunk room, the location of which I would not discover until the end of term. Now everything that was me was represented by a large bunch of shiny new keys. I owned a vast array of new things, for which I was now responsible, and they were all put away, out of sight. They were not for sharing, as things were at home. My world was represented in a single bed, on view in dormitory number four.

My parents now began to speak. For about three hours, we had worked as a team, finding out where things were, quietly placing, stowing, folding, locking. Now it was time for the inevitable parting. There was so much unsaid. This new life in boarding school was not chosen but necessary, so my being brave was an unspoken agreement. All my friends in my little primary-school sixth class of four pupils were starting boarding school life too, but in other schools.

'You'll be fine,' my mother said. 'Don't forget to write us a letter and you won't feel the time going until half-term.'

She hugged me and I could feel that she was upset. I felt embarrassed and wanted it to be over. Outside at the car, my father hugged me for a long time. 'Goodbye, love. Mind yourself and don't forget to write. We'll come and see you on Sunday week.'

There were similar scenes at other cars and I was acutely aware of being observed. I wanted my parents to go so that I could sit on my new bed and breathe. There was so much to take in. I felt as if I had been watching a fast-paced thriller at the cinema and that the interval was long overdue. Some of the events had been a blur. I couldn't remember any of the teachers' names, or those of the one or two first-year girls who had introduced themselves. I needed to stop. Recap. Calm my racing heart and look towards what would happen next. Our family car moved down the drive and they were gone. Not gone away but gone home. I was the one who'd gone away.

Fender Bender

John Piggott, Cabinteely, County Dublin

He was off his face. I didn't know what on but I knew it had to be something strong. We were standing in his gate-lodge flat. I'd just had a minor fender-bender with his (very badly parked) rusty Morris Minor.

I needed him to give me a pen and paper so we could exchange insurance details and I could get out of there. This seemed to be a major problem. If he could have kept his long, black, Christ-like hair out of his eyes for more than two seconds it might have been easier.

After some time he returned with one sheet of foolscap and a large yellow crayon. Was that all he had? Apparently so. Perhaps he'd write down his details for me and then I'd write down mine for him.

'Details, man?'

'Yes, your details – like your name and address, your insurance company, stuff like that.'

'My name?'

'Please.'

He stooped over the table and hid what he was writing like a child doing an exam. After maybe ten seconds or so, he stood up and gingerly proffered the sheet to me.

In huge yellow letters taking up most of the top half of the page he had written 'D - A - N'.

I tried to hide the smile, indeed to stifle a giggle. 'No, sorry, eh, Dan. That won't do. I need your full name.'

He took the sheet back with a sheepish shrug and an, 'Oh, ye-eah. Right.'

After some more furtive scrawling he offered it to me again. He had added, 'I - E - L'.

Reluctant Bachelors

Mary McCombs, Westport, County Mayo

My uncle Johnny was reasonably good-looking. He was of medium height and wore a cloth cap. He was going bald, a fact he did his best to disguise. He combed his hair to cover the bald spot and if any patch of scalp remained visible he would blacken it with boot polish. He was a heavy smoker, smoking Woodbines except for special occasions, when he bought Gold Flake.

He always dressed up when going into town. He was looking for a wife and he knew the pedigree of every eligible girl for miles.

He and a friend, Josie Joyce, visited my aunt's house in Mill Street. The pack of cards was produced.

'We'll play twenty-fives,' said Josie, who was also wife-hunting.

'Just the one game, then we'll read them,' was the reply.

After the game the cards were shuffled.

'Here, Josie, you box them again and cut them. We'll read yours first. This might be your lucky night.'

After the game the cards were dealt in seven groups of three, face downwards. Johnny picked them three at a time.

'There's a woman, and she's dark,' Johnny sounded conspiratorial.

'Has she money? Is she good-looking?' enquired Josie excitedly.

'There's money there all right, but I can't tell if she's good-looking. You'll meet her in the space of three.'

'This is Friday. Let me see – Saturday, Sunday, Monday, I should meet her on Monday, if it's three days. And you say she's dark. I'll be on the look-out,' said Josie. 'By the way I met Technique yesterday.'

Josie had a nickname for everyone. Technique was a lady who had buried two husbands. She appeared to attract men, even though she wasn't particularly good-looking.

Johnny spent a lot of time and energy in his search for a partner. He had set a high standard and would not consider a girl who fell short. One day he met Daddy after Mass.

'I was talking to Jim Lally the other day. He drew down a girl – a daughter of Paddy Kelly's of Knocknabo. Do you know them?' Johnny asked.

'And sure why wouldn't I know them. Paddy himself bought a heifer off me last year. He has two daughters. Which of them was mentioned?' Daddy asked.

'The one who's in the house, what does she look like? Would she be too old to have childer? Whet kind of fortune would she have?' Johnny had a barrage of questions.

'Hold your whist, man. One thing at a time. The girl in the house, did you say? She's plain enough but a good worker. There's nothing delicate about that family. She'd be no spring chicken, though, and I doubt if she'd have much of a fortune. But they're a decent family. Aren't they related to Joyces of Rossdoo that have the son a priest.' I think Daddy would have liked to see Johnny happily married.

'I missed it that I didn't marry Katie Gibbons when I had the chance. She has two fine sons now and she wasn't as bad-looking as I thought at the time. She had a fine fortune. I mightn't do as well in the long run.'

Over the years Johnny often expressed his regret at having turned down Katie because she did not have the looks, although it was rumoured that Katie was a domineering woman whose husband could never earn enough money to please her.

'When are you seeing the Kelly girl?' Daddy enquired.

'I'll be in Hogan's snug next Friday when she comes in for the commands. I'll get a good look at her on the QT.' Johnny smiled in anticipation.

The following Friday Johnny was in Hogan's snug and saw the girl for himself. Her hips were too narrow. She was not built for bearing children. If she were found to be suitable Jim Lally would have acted as go-between and found out how much of a fortune or dowry the girl would bring with her. If Johnny were satisfied, he and the girl would be introduced. Johnny was too old to go to dances and there were few matchmakers left.

Eventually he did marry – Mary, a lady from outside Castlebar. She had a cousin who had a butcher's shop in Westport. It was a happy marriage even though Mary was not young enough to have children.

The Emigrant Boat

Eddie Walsh, Nottingham (originally from County Kerry)

Autumn 1965 was a good time to be young in Ireland but not so good if you had no job, money or prospects. I had spent the previous winter in London and decided to head off there again. So I hitched from Kerry to Rosslare, unaware that at that time of year the ferry sailed only every second night. And I had picked the wrong one! I had to get a bed and breakfast in Wexford town, which left me with just enough money for the boat ticket. I arrived in Fishguard with only ten old pence. The hitching started again. A kindly Welshwoman in a van gave me half a crown which seemed a fortune to me as it fed me later.

I had a friend who was a live-in barman in a Hampstead pub so I was hoping to get a start there. After a long day of lifts I reached the outskirts of London and began using buses to get across the city, although I had to keep hopping off whenever the conductor approached.

Eventually I got to the pub. My pal let me sleep on his bedroom floor for a couple of nights. Unfortunately there was no vacancy for another barman. The only option was to go from pub to pub until an Irish guvnor who hailed from Limerick took me on. I got food and shelter as well as a job. His wife was an excellent cook and most of the customers were my fellow countrymen. Waiting a week for my first wages was a bit of a hardship but I got through it.

So don't talk to me about the recession: I do not recognise the term.

Move Over, Soccer Mom, I'm a GAA Ma!

Barbara Scully, Cabinteely, County Dublin

I don't really know what a soccer mom is... perhaps she exists only on Wisteria Lane and the like. But anyway, I am now announcing that I am happy to call myself a GAA (say it – don't spell it) Ma.

'So what,' you might say. But this is some transformation, let me tell you!

I grew up in a fairly middle-class suburb of south Dublin, where I thought that GAA was only for culchies. My three brothers had only a passing interest in sport and none whatsoever in Gaelic games of any kind. My father did take notice of GAA matches but I put that down to his advancing age and the fact that he originated from County Laois. No, in our house GAA was uncool and something to be ignored at all costs.

So now I find myself still living in south county Dublin, mother of three daughters – no sons. From the time they were born I was delighted to have an 'all girl' team of kids and was relieved that I would never have to feign interest in anything other than the odd game of tennis or basketball. We weren't exactly a Barbie house but sport was not really on the agenda.

Then middle daughter discovered football – Gaelic football. Initially it was a summer camp run by the local club which would keep the two younger girls busy for a week! I happily swallowed my ancient bias and signed them up. Youngest put in the week and was visibly relieved when it was over. Too much mud and mess for her liking. But for middle daughter...it was love at first kick, or throw-in, or whatever.

She begged to be allowed to join the local club and soon began to play on a team. My heart sank. The prospect of hours on the sideline of a football pitch filled me, and him, with dread. We had weekly rows about who would draw the short straw and get to 'do the football'. And then there was training. More shivering on an exposed pitch which used to be a landfill site (I kid you not).

But slowly the GAA began to work its magic. At the end of that first season, the team was taken off for 'dinner' in the local burger place. Then there was the prize-giving ceremony at which my daughter proudly took her place with her team-mates and was praised for her commitment to the club and the game. My heart was full.

That was four years ago. She is now a member of our local club's under-12s and we are old hands at this GAA thing. We have played matches north, south and west of Dublin and the craic of lining up at the local church car park for the 'big trip to wherever' and the debates on whether to go via the M50 or a more traditional route is pure entertainment.

We have made sorties further afield, to Trim and to Ashbourne, where we were stunned by the facilities of the local GAA clubs. Standing on the pristine pitch in Trim, coming up to 8pm on a beautiful May evening last year, I remember thinking that this was a grand way to pass such an evening, especially when we had just won the match! Then, as we prepared the convoy to head back to the big smoke, we were told that our club had brought a picnic for us all and we should meet up by the castle. And so it was that I found myself in the company of the other GAA mums and dads, in the shadow of the medieval walls of Trim Castle, tucking into a picnic of epic proportions, as the light drained from the sky. There was a hint of decadence and indulgence and joy in the air!

And I fell in love: with the game (the scoring still gets me sometimes) and with the ethos of this organisation. With the passion and commitment of volunteers who take my daughter (along with thousands of kid all around the country) and teach her the skills needed for the game and the value of teamwork as well as building her confidence.

So I share this in case your child shows some interest in the local GAA summer camp, Go for it, I say! It could be the start of something beautiful.

A Kansas City Phone Call to an Irish Mother

Liam Daly, Dublin

– Hi
– Hello?
– It's me, one of your children
– Oh, hello, me –
– It's raining pretty heavy here so I just thought I'd give you a ring instead of going out with the dog.
– It's lashing here too.
– We've got the ice stuff, you know that freezing rain ice-storm business?
– Oh, it's freezin' here too.
– No I mean actual ice.
– It's very icy here too.
– Yeah, but outside the window here right now there are two rabbits, a cat, and a small woman frozen rigid, completely shrouded in ice. They might not be thawed for Christmas.
– That's terrible.
– Yes, the temperature is way below freezing.
– It's very cold here too.
– But we have a real feel of twenty degrees below freezing.
– I know, we have the heating on high.
– But for us the weird thing is that it was hot the last few days.
– You know, it was the same here.
– Ma, it doesn't get that hot in Ireland in summer, never mind the end of November.
– I know, it's all gone crazy if you ask me.

- It was really warm here, as in T-shirt weather.
- It was very warm here too. We had to turn the heating down low. Your father was wearing a T-shirt
- It was one-hundred-and-sixty-three degrees Fahrenheit here.
- Your father would know what it was here; it was awful warm though, very close.
- Ma, it wasn't. It was one-hundred-and-sixty-three degrees.
- Oh you know me, I don't understand these different temperature things.
- Well it was five times the heat that Ireland gets on its hottest day in the year.
- Oh that's too hot; you couldn't live like that.
- No, we should be grateful for the cold spell, I suppose.
- You sound tired.
- I'm grand.
- Have you been to bed?
- Yes.
- When did you go to bed?
- Ma, I'm a grown man. I've even grown sideways.
- When did you go to bed?
- I don't have a bed.
- Well, when did you go to sleep?
- August.
- No wonder you're sick.
- I'm not sick.
- Well you don't sound well.
- I'm grand.
- Are you eating properly?
- This is America; nobody eats properly.
- You have to eat.
- I do eat.
- You have to eat enough.
- No, I have to eat less. How do you think I grew sideways?

- You're an awful man.
- So I hear.
- How is work?
- Very busy.
- Have you cut your hair?
- I combed it last week.
- Why don't you cut your hair. It looks nice when it's cut.
- There's no need; it cuts itself.
- Don't be daft, your hair can't cut itself.
- It does, I have self-cutting hair. It grows all manky, splits and breaks off.
- You're impossible.
- How's brother the youngest's hair?
- Oh, it's awful. It reaches down to the back of his knees now.
- Is he planning on selling it?
- I wish he'd do something with it.
- Maybe he's thinking of learning to play music.
- No, he didn't say anything about music and he tells his mother everything.
- Perhaps he has a girlfriend?
- What would he be doing with a girlfriend?
- I can't imagine.
- You know such-and-such?
- Nope, I never heard of such-and-such.
- Ah you do, it's so-and-so's little sister.
- I don't know so-and-so.
- You do, of course, it's missus what's–her–face's eldest. She went to school in that place where that fella used to go.
- Oh, so-and-so, yeah, I know who you mean.
- Well, it's terrible but such-and-such is after getting pregnant.
- I think you'll be OK.
- But it's really terrible, you know? Missus what's-her-face is in bits.

- Well it wasn't me.
- Don't be saying that.
- Well, it wasn't; I was in America.
- I hope you're not getting any of those girls over there into trouble.
- You haven't told me how to yet.
- Well, I can't talk here all day. I have to get the dinner on for your father. Would you like to have a word with him?
- I can't right now, I need to defrost the dog.
- Bye for now, then.
- Goodbye so.

Belfast Brick

Francesca Walsh, County Wicklow

Red-brick streets oiled with rain hid the tailor's shop in the shadow of a red Belfast church. The stranger had asked a young girl serving in a haberdashery where she might find a shop selling yarn. The girl, in answering the question, made certain that her own background and her distance from the location and from that other side were well known.

'There's a shop two streets across from here on the street beside the chapel or cathedral or whatever it is.'

It was no cathedral but one of three red-brick houses of worship where generations of separation had been nurtured. Ignorance and poverty saw to that.

The tailor's shop was a small room with a high counter, a glass separator atop the counter, marking out the smallest office imaginable. There was a tariff for repairs – skirts, jackets, coats – all worth their measure. This was the place where thrift was a necessity, not a virtue. In the back someone sewed not for pleasure but for the few pounds. When the stranger went in, trumpeted by a bell, the woman of the shop was leaning against her high altar listening. Her eyes, but nothing else, acknowledged the visitor.

'They're getting married next year.' The speaker had no accent that marked her out to the stranger's ear and nothing that marked her to the eye. Hers was the same singsong voice rising and falling like any other the stranger had heard in the town. No doubt had she been local, the stranger could have told the street where the speaker was from, if indeed it was a street.

A look might have told the trained observer everything else they needed to know but the stranger saw nothing. The woman who was speaking was not alone. She had two children with her, a boy and a girl. He was about ten, she looked a little older. Both were dressed neatly, respectably for the time. Both still, listening to their mother with the polite lack of interest of ones who'd heard the story more than once.

The woman who was speaking repeated her words to the woman of the shop for emphasis.

'They're getting married next year. They're fifteen now but they'll be sixteen by then,' she said, nodding to make sure the woman of the shop understood the significance.

If she did, the woman of the shop gave no sign; she simply carried on listening. The stranger listened too.

The conversation continued for a short time with arcane references to a 'she'. It appeared to the stranger that the nameless 'she' had in some way organised or at least connived at the marriage to be celebrated the following year. The stranger was embarrassed to be so close to the intimate details of lives of people she would never meet, though their very anonymity gave the intrusion a cloak of decency.

The stranger thought now that she should forget the wool and simply leave the shop woman and her guest to their confidences. As she made up her mind to go, as invisibly as she could, the mother of the two hushed children suddenly made her own move to go. She turned to the woman of the shop and pointed to the boy, who gave no reaction.

'She made a match for him too but I said no.' Then she left, not waiting for a reply.

The stranger left the shop and walked two red-brick streets back to Donegall Place to the traffic and the bustle of the shoppers, to the flashing lights and the cries of the mobile phones.

Good Grief

Lyn Duff, Shankill, County Dublin

Being a family of cat lovers, we missed the cats we left behind in South Africa but as we had taken a few years to settle down in Ireland, it was quite some time before we decided to add that feline dimension to our home. An unfulfilled longing on my part and sustained nagging on the children's part eventually tipped the scale. CoCo, our male cat, came from the Blue Cross, and Fizzle, the female, from the DSPCA. A pet each for our son and daughter: pigeon pairs, as it were.

A short while later Fizzle went missing. The last time we saw her she was licking dinner off her whiskers before bounding up to the window. One paw raised, ears cocked and eyes scanning the garden for any sign of danger, she sat on the edge of the windowsill. Then, in one fluid, elegant movement, she leapt away and was gone.

When she didn't come in for breakfast the next morning, I didn't worry too much. Like all cats, she generally did whatever she pleased. By lunchtime I was concerned; by bedtime, worried and mildly frantic. She had never missed more than one meal in the few months she had been with us. Early the next day I started calling her, banging her plate and looking under bushes and in unlikely places: the old broken-down dog kennel under the hedge, the enticingly warm hot press, even in the attic in the doubtful hope that she had somehow got in there. But no miaow.

I printed up a whole lot of notices and sent my son around our road to deliver them. The note begged people to check their outhouses and garages, to tell us anything, even if the news was bad. The note ended: 'Missing cat, sad family.' Still nothing.

Then, a few days later, a neighbour came around. Early one morning the previous week she had seen the refuse collection truck loading up the body of a little brown cat on the main road opposite the Italian chippie. My husband went up to check with the owners of the chippie: Yes, they had seen a little cat struck by a car on Tuesday night. The night she went missing.

So that was it – no doubt.

Isn't it strange what the death of a pet does to us? I tried to reason with myself, 'It's only an animal. Warm-blooded and living, yes, but not a person. Nothing like the death of a human being. Not the same thing at all.'

But I caught myself thinking of the way she used to sit after giving herself a thorough wash-and-brush-up: the tip of her pink tongue poking out from between her teeth, regarding us with a comical air. The way she purr-miaowed when talking to us. How she would curl up in a snug bundle, nose buried in paws and only her dreaming, twitching whiskers showing. The sheer beauty of her brown-speckled ugliness and the messy marmalade smear across her nose. Her obvious joy when playing with the children, chasing a bright ribbon with a feather tied all wonkily, but still enticingly, at the end. When she finally caught the feather, she would delicately pick it up in her mouth and carry it under the nearest chair or table and lie there, paw resting possessively on her 'prey'. She was an edgy, excitable bundle of energy, ready to turn play into pounce at a whisker's notice.

I'd shake myself out of this downhill reverie and crossly say: 'For goodness' sake, it's just an animal, a super-independent cat: they don't feel anything for us!' But those sneaky little sadnesses kept hiding around corners, waiting to jump out at unexpected moments.

At night she'd snuggle up to me in bed, lying in the crook

of my legs and preventing me from stretching out with the tenderest of claws dug delicately into my foot. At the same time she'd lullaby me to sleep with the softest of purrs.

Yes, I was exasperated at times, when she and our other cat would play 'Pounce on Thy Neighbour' in the early hours of the morning: The sneaky pouncer would creep upstairs and spring on to the unlucky pouncee who was usually sleeping on my bed, spitting and hissing with great gusto. My husband and I would wake up nearly vertical, practically hovering in mid-air, our hearts hammering in fright.

And I vividly, malodorously, remember when we first collected her from the DSPCA: she was so terrified on the trip home that she first threw up, then messed herself. This left me with the unenviable task of cleaning up a panicky, stinky cat. And then her carrier.

But still, I loved her. We all did. She was part of our lives and deserved every bit of our grief. Our cat, our friend, Fizz.

All Set for D-Day

Kathy McDevitt, Greystones, County Wicklow

Claire stood for a long time peering through the toy shop window, her two hands outstretched on the grimy glass. A fog patch pulsed on the cold surface in front of her mouth. She had passed this window every day since starting school, on turning four, the previous November, and she could recite by heart the position and price of every toy in the display. The wooden dolls' house £7/2s/3d, above that the Hornby train set, a whopping £9/10s and, in front of that, the basket of marbles, ten for threepence.

Today there was a new addition to the display. In the centre of the window stood the most beautiful doll Claire had ever seen. She was a fifteen-inch high Crolly doll with long blonde hair that sparkled in the sunlight. She wore a red plaid pleated skirt and a cream cable-knit sweater. She had white ankle socks and little black T-strap shoes. Claire could just see her two front teeth through slightly parted lips and the cutest dimples in the middle of her kneecaps. Her name was Susie. Her arms and legs moved and she closed her eyes when she was lying down. Claire knew all this because it said so on the box. She stared at Susie for so long she saw her wink at her with her magnificent, heavy-lashed eye, made of clear blue glass.

Claire knew then that no matter what it took, Susie had to be hers. She gasped at the hand-written, luminous green price-card stuck on the front of the box and said aloud, '£3/15s'. That's when Mrs Murphy poked her head out the open shop door and said, 'Hurry on home now, Claire Brennan. Your mother will be wondering where you are.'

Claire took down her heavy piggy-bank the minute she got in the door and prised the rubber stopper out of the bottom. She shook the contents out on to her bed. She had one £1 note. It had the picture of a very pretty woman on one side and a big building on the other. She had twelve silver stampeding bulls, and five brown flying chickens. She spent ages working it out but she thought this came to £2 pounds and five pence, leaving her £1/14/7d short. She had just over half the amount she needed. Even if she gave up the peg's legs, liquorice sherbets and banana rock at the school tuck shop for a whole year she would never make up the difference. Christmas wasn't long over and her birthday was not until next November. It was hopeless.

Walking slowly past the shop front the next day, Claire didn't stop. She couldn't bear to look in. She was sure Susie was following her with her please-take-me-home eyes. She broke into a run and didn't stop until she was in the front door. Her mother could see Claire's misery and soon got out of her what was on her mind. Full of can-do gusto, her mother reminded her of the fancy dress competition she and her sister were to take part in on Saturday at the annual school fundraiser. If they could come up with a fantastic costume they would be in with a good chance of winning a substantial cash prize. 'And I have an idea that might go down very well with the judges,' said her mother.

Over the next few days the Brennans worked hard at putting together the fancy dress costumes. Large cardboard boxes and rolls of tinfoil were procured. The cardboard was flattened, cut into shapes, taped, reinforced and covered in layers of tinfoil. Claire hadn't a clue what the costume was about but her mother said it was brilliant and she trusted her.

Passing the shop on Friday afternoon Claire noticed something about the display was different. On Susie's box, under the price card marked £3/15s was a new white card with another price on it. £9.00 it shouted. She looked at the train set and the dolls' house. Every toy had a 'new' and much bigger price on it. A knot formed in Claire's stomach and a lump rose to her throat. Even if they won the first prize at the fancy dress she would never have anywhere near £9. No matter how long her mother explained that this was new money but the same value as the old money Claire just couldn't grasp what she meant. After tea, Claire's mother sat her down and put all her coins out in front of her and counted. 'Two pounds and five pence in old money is the same as four pounds and eighty-five pence in new money. If the new price for Susie is nine pounds you need to win at least four pounds and fifteen pence at the fancy dress.'

On the day of the fancy dress Claire and her sister took their place in the line-up of contestants. They were dressed up as two huge new fifty-pence pieces, which they wore like sandwich boards. Claire carried a sign on a piece of card on a stick saying 'All set for D-Day'. Claire knew the costumes were good by the reactions people were giving them. In circles they paraded past the judges, who eventually made a shortlist of winners. Third prize of two new pounds went to the Tin Man from Oz. Four new pounds went to Bo-peep and her sheep. Claire could hardly breathe. It was all or nothing now. Susie was coming home or risked going to some other girl's home. She couldn't bear the thought. Then the announcement came over the loudspeakers: 'The 1971 fancy dress first prize of six new pounds goes to entry number 23, "All Set for D-Day", Mary and Claire Brennan.' Claire leapt into the air as best she could under the weight of the costume. Mother was right again.

Claire wanted to go to the toy shop there and then but she had to wait until Monday. The school bell rang and Claire ran out of the school gates, not even waiting to meet up with her sister. When she passed the toy-shop window she stopped dead in her tracks. The place where Susie had stood all week was empty. Susie was gone. 'Too late, I was too late', was all she could repeat to herself over and over again. It felt like the end of the world for Claire. She let her head go blank and walked home blindly. She burst in the front door and fell into her mother's arms. Mother carried her to the kitchen and there on the table smiling back at her through her cellophane window was Susie.

Tide-Turning

Adrienne Troy, Greystones, County Wicklow

It is summer 2008. There are six of us, my daughters Jen, thirteen, and Danielle, twelve, my son Stephen, seven, my Dad Des, my Mum Phyllis and myself. We are on a beach called Les Sables Vigniers on Oléron island in the south-west of France.

The tide is rising and the height and strength of the waves is increasing as each wave lifts lots of people off their feet. There is a collective roar of excitement. An orange flag flies, signalling that the water is safe to swim in but care has to be taken.

I stand up. 'Let's go home,' I say, stretching.

Des looks longingly at the sea. 'I fancy another dip.'

The waves are strong, I warn him.

'I'm not an aul fella yet!' he says and does a mock-geriatric shuffle along the sand, then jogs jauntily down to the sea, looking fit and obviously feeling strong. Danielle whips off her beach dress. "If Dessie is getting in, so am I!' she says and sprints in after him.

They wait to time the waves as the water is being sucked out. In they dash and they are instantly lifted up and begin bobbing along with the others. Suddenly Danielle disappears from sight, Mum says, 'I can't see her any more!' Jen runs to the water's edge. I stare at all the heads in the sea, trying to locate Danielle's blonde head. No sign.

Then Des goes in deeper. Danielle has shouted to him that she is being dragged and can't swim in. They move about fifty feet to the right. We watch helplessly. I remember the sounds all around – voices, my son, my Mum. I feel so responsible. I want to rewind time. I want my husband Alan to be here. He is due to arrive in two days.

They appear briefly, then go underwater. Des reaches Danielle and tries to lift her towards the shore. Trying to propel her to safety, having no lifesaving experience whatsoever, he ends up pushing himself further underwater. A wave comes and he gets caught in the swell. The waves are huge and thunder in with a deafening crash.

Jen tries to get in to them but the waves knock her down. People are stumbling and being helped out of the water. We are at the shoreline. People are shouting and calling out all around us. My stomach is gripped by a tight feeling of sheer terror. I have a lump in my throat and I can feel unshed tears in my eyes. I keep reassuring myself with the mantra: 'They will get out, they will come back, and we will all go home today.'

A man tries to rescue Des, whose arms are flailing madly in the water. He gives up. Another man reaches him with a bodyboard. He hits him hard on the shoulder and speaks sternly in French. Des holds the man's arm and is brought to shore. Another man throws Danielle a board and reels her in.

Des is being carried along by two big men. As he and Danielle meet, they hug each other and Des's legs begin to give way. The six of us hug and relief washes over us. I guide him to the towel to lie down.

He goes blue and is shivering. A feeling of unease grips me. His teeth are chattering and people rush over with offers of help. Jen runs to get the lifeguards. Jen, Danielle and Stevie sit at Des's head. They are all crying. Danielle keeps saying, 'You saved me, Dessie,' and stroking his brow. I feel so relieved that they are out of the water but am terrified that he will die on the beach.

Des is stretchered off the beach and goes by ambulance to hospital. He is discharged that night following chest x-rays and scans. When I think of that day, I feel that we were so lucky that we all got to go home that night. It could have ended so differently. Dad risked his life for my daughter.

The Other Side

S. O'Dwyer, Kilkenny

She sat in the lobby waiting, wanting to run away. The waiting area had high ceilings and was painted off-white matt. She had read somewhere that cream was a soothing and tranquil colour. The lattice blinds were drawn over the windows of what she supposed were offices. The place didn't smell as she imagined it would. It smelled of pine. She looked at the bright red of the dying poinsettia. It was early January. The muted sound of a radio could be heard somewhere.

She sat with her head down, her parents sitting across from her. She couldn't raise her eyes to meet theirs but she knew her mother was crying. She made the choking sound she always made when she was hurting. She pulled her eyes away from the faux-vintage rug on the floor, trying not to acknowledge the guilt and rising panic, and met her father's eyes. He was staring stoically ahead with a stiff upper lip. He held her mother's hand. She had never seen her parents holding hands before.

The early evening dying light filtered through a chipped lattice blind. Little flecks of dust landed on the transparent plastic sack. Her name was written in black permanent marker. The hospital had already sent it over. Through the plastic she could make out her wet jeans and T-shirt. The sack was fogged up with the wet clothes. Her runners! She couldn't see them, then she remembered...she had taken them off. The ends of her jeans had been heavy and sodden and dragged her down but she'd kept them on. Even then she had been thinking of decency and what people would think. The absurdity of it. She almost laughed out loud.

She was ashamed, disgusted and still in shock, ashamed of what she'd put them through. Sorry to be here with them, sorry to...be. This wasn't what she had thought. She looked up. Her mother had her head in her hands. Beginning at her toes, guilt started a cold, almost numbing journey up to her consciousness. She felt alone, even now. It's true she thought, that one can be surrounded by people and still feel so achingly alone. No one had judged her. In fact, they spoke to her almost as if she was a child, putting their arm around her shoulder, leading her... somewhere. She couldn't really remember clearly. It was a bit hazy. She was very cold. They had put her on a bed – well it wasn't really a bed, more like a trolley thing that had railings on the side that they pulled up. They took her clothes off, gently helping her to pull her T-shirt over her head. They took her underwear off and gave her a pale blue gown with no back, just a cord below the back of her neck. The nurse had helped her to tie it on as she was too cold to stretch that far behind. She was cold, very cold. They gave her a plastic cup of water and two little pink tablets. She wouldn't take them, she'd had enough of pills, and besides, they didn't sedate the pain or emptiness. She asked where the toilet was. A nurse followed her in and led her back to the 'bed'. The curtains of the cubicle weren't drawn. Everyone could see her but no one spoke to her. She had always hated the smell of wet wool. It was there, on her skin and in her nose, although they had taken her jumper away...somewhere, wherever they put these things. Wet wool smelled like old ladies and must.

They couldn't do any more with her. Their work was done. She was warmer and dry. They took her temperature in the ambulance, 'Love, how long were you in the water? Do you remember? OK, OK, don't worry, it's OK.' She tried to remember but her brain wouldn't allow it. She shivered as if she was cold to the marrow. Her skin, which was usually milk-bottle white, had turned a bluish shade. She really needed to go to the toilet again.

She looked up above her mother's head at the flat-screen TV, which was playing SKY News on a loop. She was mesmerised by the moving images on the screen. One of the pine doors opened, and a lady of about forty-five with greying hair and glasses called her name. She nodded. She put her arms around her. Her parents stood up to follow them into the office. 'It's OK. It's not necessary for the family to be present at this point. Please take a seat. It won't take too long.'

They later put her in a wheelchair – a wheelchair! – with what she presumed was her file on her lap. It was in a brown manila envelope, sealed with a little white label. On it was typed her name, date of birth and date of admission. Oh God! A male nurse – maybe a doctor but most likely a nurse – appeared from the ether, introduced himself and hung the plastic bag containing her things over one of the handles of the wheelchair. He wheeled her down a corridor and turned left: 'Off we go'. He began talking about *American Idol* or some other such stuff in a vain attempt to distract her. They came to a stop before a heavy pine door. He swiped a card over a keypad, then pressed a buzzer beside it. A heavy-set nurse who wouldn't look out of place in *One Flew over the Cuckoo's Nest* let them in, closing the heavy pine door with a slam. Well that's Ratched.

She would soon discover that most of the others in the ward joked about that movie. It was a way of dealing with the regime of the day and the situation they were in. Very few people would ever experience this, would never know about the slow shifting of time inside, sleeping during the day only to be awoken by the clattering of the tea trolley, lukewarm water and weak tea, the endless hours transfixed in front of the coloured images on the screen, the board games put high on a shelf and never taken down, people pacing like caged animals, staring into the middle distance. The most frightening thing was the heavy pine partition deliberately indistinguishable from the wall, which was pulled across to separate the male and female patients in times of 'high distress' – patients on the verge of acts of violence against staff or other patients but most often against themselves.

She would experience the meetings between nurse and patient, doctor and patient, nurses and doctors meeting about the patient. Monitoring, observing, checking and noting sleep and eating habits, sociable or loner, aggressive, passive, passive-aggressive. Everything noted every fifteen minutes. Decisions would be made for her: when to eat, what to eat, how to dress. There were regulation pyjamas with no strings on the waist, the only difference between patients being the colours of pyjamas. Hers were brighter, like the girl in the foetal position who never spoke but cried whenever the nurses wanted her to eat and the older man who took his off and said inappropriate and embarrassing things when they were eating like, 'I've never had a girlfriend. I have nobody to fuck.' Male nurses took him under each arm, led him back to his room, across from the station – glass, no privacy. Nobody away from here knew and would ever know what goes on. What will haunt and hurt for life and leave one shuddering for days like after a nightmare that lasts anything between four and sixteen weeks.

She would learn about the staff, those liked and respected and those disliked, like the night nurses who turned the main lights off too early and gave the night medication and 'sleepers' before they were meant to so as not to be bothered during the first coffee break of their shift; those who wouldn't allow them to have their coffee at 8.30pm if they didn't eat all their tea at 5.00; the ones who opened the door to the enclosed courtyard for the bare twenty minutes a day and not at all during the weekend. She would discover that there are those with a sixth sense who would never cajole or make someone talk; they encouraged but wouldn't shelter you from the reality. In other wards one nurse to three patients; here one nurse to each patient. It was important for the nurses not to be seen as favouring one patient over another. Few felt that they belonged there. Some were so sick and out of it, through a combination of drugs and voluntary mental death, that they had given up. There are worse deaths than physical death, she learned.

There was no option but to succumb to the regime. 8.30 breakfast, 12.30pm dinner, tea at 5.00pm, sometimes 4.30pm. Medication after meals. The night medication, standing at the nurses' station. Plastic cups of water, waiting in the queue, more little pills, swallow before turning to leave. They watched everything. Sometimes called you back just 'to be sure'. The careful counting and monitoring of it. One calling and checking, one doling it all out. The staff changed at 8 o'clock. The fifteen-minute night checks. What could you possibly do in fifteen minutes? It seemed absurd to her until someone told her about the girl who shattered her brain by hitting her head against the bathroom tiles. She died in thirteen minutes.

Her parents were already inside the door when she arrived. They weren't holding hands any more. Vacant but curious faces watched the new girl being wheeled in. Most had arrived the same way. Others came in under doctor and garda escort. They could see her looking at the fish tank, the circle of chairs, a muted TV. There were four men, one girl, probably in her early twenties, curled up on a chair in the foetal position. 'This will be your room. You're nice and near the nurses' station if you need anything during the night. There's a bell here on the wall. Look. There's another one in your bathroom.' No locks on the doors, except the main door, closely watched, glass, ground-floor ward, plastic vases, no sharp edges anywhere. She later found out that there were plastic cups and plates too. Sweet Jesus. I should not be here. She said a silent prayer. She hadn't spoken to Jesus since…before. If you ever loved me you would let me escape the never-ending pain, the emptiness that comes from not knowing yourself, from self-hatred, loss, guilt and fear.

Her parents struggled to understand, looking at her as if they don't know her, her mother with a sharp intake of breath. A female nurse had brought them through the public door, their daughter wheeled through another door, separated from them for the first time. They looked around in terror, seeing only the curious faces and the large number of nurses watching. Yet it's nobody's fault: a series of knocks from life together with poor coping strategies and an inability to communicate. They could see the on-call doctor writing up his notes in the little glass office behind the nurses' station. This is where their daughter would be. This is the place society deemed appropriate for people like her. Her father turned around to face the wall, then went out to wait in the corridor, not knowing what else to do, where else to be. He did not know how his daughter felt. It was totally outside his frame of reference. He could not even try to understand it: the pain kept getting in the way, pushing all other thoughts out of his head. Her life was their life.

Although they had assured them that they would look after her, when he looked into his daughter's eyes he too realised that spiritual death hurts a lot more than physical death.

Search for a School Motto

Alan Cox, Dublin

Our school recently had the dreaded Whole School Inspection. It's actually a very painless process and very positive for a school but it does require an enormous amount of paperwork and, as part of this, we suddenly found we had to produce a comprehensive document called the 'school plan'.

This wasn't a difficult task, as the policies and the subject plans were all in place – it just took a weekend to pull it together. Which we did very successfully. But when the ninety-five-page document was completed, one thing seemed to be missing…

A motto.

Every school plan we'd seen had a motto on the front. Something profound in Latin. Something that encapsulated what the school stood for, what it was about.

We didn't.

We felt a bit inadequate.

Something had to be done…

So we came up with a motto. Of sorts.

My wife made the comment that with all the fundraising for sports facilities in recent years, the school motto should be 'Let's Build a Sports Hall!' To her horror I rather liked it. While she protested that she was only joking and would I ever stop being silly, I began racking my brains to find the remnants of my Inter Cert Latin. 'Constructare' meant 'Build', that was a start. 'Domus' was 'house', and I remembered at some sports events the title of 'victor ludorum' was awarded to the winner of the games. So a motto of 'Constructare Domus Ludorum' seemed a pretty good approximation of 'Let's Build a House of Sport'. I took a deep breath and printed out the School Plan, emblazoned with this very fine motto.

Two days later, I handed three copies of the school plan to the inspectors. It was going well. I showed a copy to Peter, a good-humoured member of the parents' association and told him what the motto meant.

The following day, Peter emailed me, in a state of some consternation. There was a problem. Apparently, 'Domus Ludorum' doesn't mean 'House of Sport'; it means 'House of Games'. And the games the Romans were talking about here were of the 'fun and games' variety that really wouldn't be appropriate for a modern Irish secondary education. Our motto actually translated as 'Let's Build a Brothel'.

Later that day, the chief inspector chattily asked me about the motto – he'd studied Latin in school himself but couldn't remember much of it, or work out what our motto meant. I muttered something about 'educating the whole person', talked at length about the origins of the school crest and hastily took him for lunch in Hunter's Hotel.

The inspection went very well indeed.

The Liar

Kathryn Crowley, Dublin (formerly Killarney, County Kerry)

My parents were living in two rooms behind a small shop in Main Street in Killarney when my eldest brother Liam was born in July 1956. My mother described him as a 'whirlwind'. He was full of energy, always climbing, exploring, shouting loudly and generally getting into mischief. When he was a baby, everything had to be moved out of his reach. As a toddler, he was a danger to himself and, despite my mother's best efforts, he was involved in many minor incidents and accidents.

Kieran was born in October 1957 and, by all accounts, was the complete opposite. He slept serenely for hours at a stretch. He woke to be fed and to be changed and then he settled down happily again to sleep soundly. He had little or no interest in expending energy either in trying to walk or trying to talk. By the age of eighteen months, he had not attempted to do either. My mother didn't know whether to be relieved or anxious.

When she went out to work in our shop, she wheeled Kieran's pram to a spot behind the cash drawer, where he mostly just slept or lay quietly looking around him. The customers and neighbours all had an opinion.

'What is he now? Seven months? He should be pulling himself up to sit by now!'

'Twelve months and no attempt to walk yet! I wouldn't like that now. Sure, my Bríd was walking the full length of the kitchen at eleven months.'

'And has he said anything yet? Anything at all? I remember

well, your Liam was all talk at that age.'

When Liam turned three, the nuns from the Mercy Convent came looking for him to enrol him in Junior Infants. They needed to make up numbers and, more importantly, to put names in roll books for when the *cigire* [inspector] called. My mother was happy to have him out from under her feet for a few hours and sent him off to 'big' school to burn up some of his energy.

When he arrived home from school after his first day, he bounded in through the shop and straight into the back kitchen where Kieran was just waking from a snooze. Liam was anxious to try out the new phrase he had learned in the schoolyard earlier that day. When Kieran, then twenty-one months old, smiled up at him mutely, Liam leaned into the play-pen and said, 'Anyway, you're only a feckin' liar!'

My mother had come in behind him from the shop and heard Liam's pronouncement on his younger brother. She was wryly amused. 'I wish!' she said to my father when she was relating the story to him later that evening. They discussed whether they should send Kieran 'to see someone', though they were not exactly sure who the 'someone' might be.

You have to be careful what you wish for. Kieran had been biding his time. He was waiting until he could walk steadily before he put his feet under him. At twenty-three months he got up one day and walked all the way from the kitchen door out to the front door of the shop. He had obviously also decided that he would speak in full sentences before he would vocalise. Two weeks later, at breakfast, the feckin' liar spoke for the first time and stunned everyone by saying, 'Can I have the cornflakes please?'

Irish Resourcefulness – With A Sting in the Tail

Jerry Purcell, Dún Laoghaire, County Dublin

Tribunals, independent reports, commissions, investigative panels…Ireland is currently gripped in the feverish pursuit of wrongdoing, bad decisions, cover-up and fudge. Deep inside, we all know this is an exercise performed more for the spirit of the chase than the kill – we don't really *do* justice.

Such distaste for punishing those who take an inventive approach to the laws and rules of the land is not really on. But, you see, we were born to be resourceful. There's no point in denying it or shame in admitting it. The Irish citizen has a genetically hard-wired ability to find the quickest, easiest and most ingenious solution to any problem, with a general ambivalence towards quality. If there was a national motto on our tricolour, it would read, 'Sure, it'll be grand.'

As often as not, our predisposition towards the short cut or the sidestep leads us to regret, remorse and double the work at triple the cost. But not always. Our resourcefulness can be elegant and effective, brutally simple and straight to the point.

My true story of Irish resourcefulness concerns a family friend for many years. Now retired, he was a Garda, the gentleman sort of Garda who seems to have been decommissioned along with the blue serge, silver-buttoned uniform.

He was called – on a Friday night many years ago – to a bar where a punter was getting a bit out of control. By the time our hero arrived, the punter had smashed a mirror, stolen the barman's watch and threatened several regulars. He was drunk, belligerent and about 6'3" in old money.

Our Garda friend managed to get him into the squad car and was instructed by the sergeant on duty not to take him to the cells but to bring him home. The drunken hulk's house was out in the country and entered by a broken-down gateway with a half-built wall.

No sooner had the car stopped in the drive than the drunk jumped out. He lurched over to the many concrete blocks on the ground and picked one up. Just as he hefted the block at the squad car, our hero let the clutch out and spun the car out of harm's way. This was getting out of hand. The drunk was bending down for another block and our Garda was on his own, miles from the station and at a serious physical disadvantage.

What to do? What to do? An NYPD cop would already have his taser or his 38mm out of the holster. Game over. Even a British bobby could lug out the baton and restore a bit of 'propah ordah' if necessary. But our hero had the standard-issue weapon of every Irish citizen. Resourcefulness.

He quickly scanned the battleground, before sidestepping the next concrete missile. Then, as the drunk swung off-balance, our Garda seized his chance. Grabbing the man's belt, he pulled the drunk's trousers down to his ankles. 'What the…' the drunk must have cursed, before his fate became clear.

'Ah no, not the nettles!'

There's often a sting in the tail when you take a shortcut to solve a problem. And it's usually deserved.

Football Confession

Conal Brennan, Greystones, County Wicklow

It was early April and I was at morning soccer training. I was a coach for the team and I was working with my daughter to help her with her kick-outs as she was the goalie. She was kicking the ball out to me and I was kicking it back to her. One of her booming kick-outs was sailing past me so I back-pedalled to try to catch the ball and I collided with the floodlight pole. The pain and the small trickle of blood were bad enough. But worse were the giggles emanating from Shauna. I let my daughter know that I did not appreciate her laughter. I looked around to see if anyone else had witnessed my poor reversing – luckily there were no further witnesses and I reckoned that I had got away with it.

Sadly my hurt pride was not going to be given time to heal. Two weeks later Shauna was at Saturday evening Mass and the priest said that he would hear Confessions after Mass. As Shauna was making her Confirmation soon it was suggested that she go along. As with most people, she was under pressure to come up with a suitable sin to confess to. So when the priest asked her she told him that she had laughed at her father. 'Why?' he innocently asked? 'He ran into a pole,' was the reply. Thinking that I had crashed my car into an ESB pole, the priest asked for further information and when the full story was revealed the confessor and confessee laughed in unison. Now my embarrassment was complete.

The Family Shop

Ethel Corduff, London (formerly Tralee, County Kerry)

We had a small shop at the poorer end of the main street, ironically called Upper Castle Street. The important end with the banks and big shops was called Lower Castle Street! Our little shop was what was often called a huckster's shop, selling anything and everything: bread, buns, ice-cream, sweets, fruit, small groceries and dilisk (edible seaweed) which was gathered and dried on the seashore, often by us children. We also sold periwinkles, cooked in our kitchen in a big pot with a whole packet of salt. Vegetables were usually bought from relatives who had farms outside the town. Farmers' wives would bring in eggs and exchange them for tea and sugar on Sunday mornings after Mass.

Bread was the most important food in the 1940s, especially as it was very scarce during and after the war years. I remember when I was about three and a half, being hidden behind the counter while Mammy served customers. When Mammy replied to a woman who was not a regular customer that we did not have any bread, I piped up, 'Oh, yes we have!' which must have been very embarrassing.

My father did not like the shop – after all he had worked on a ship and had even tried to get work as an actor in Hollywood – but he liked to introduce a new idea. I must have been about eight when Thompson's, a big bakery in Cork city, over sixty miles away, started making sliced bread. It created a huge interest. My father, who was the only man in County Kerry who read the *Manchester Guardian*, quickly heard about this and contacted

Thompson's. I am not sure how he did that because making phone calls was rare then and only the bigger shops had phones.

Soon we were one of the first shops in our town to have sliced bread delivered from Cork. I was so excited on Tuesdays and Thursdays because the big Thompson's van pulled up outside and the bread was lugged into the shop in a big basket. People queued up to buy it and we had to ration it to two loaves per customer.

The Door

Majella Reid, Longford (formerly County Mayo)

I dropped the wheelbarrow on the cement path and jumped at the abrupt sound it made. My blackened hands rising to my hips, I turned and looked back through the side gate of our house.

'Are you coming or not?' I called out.

'Not.'

'Gracie, the fire will go out.'

'I'm not supposed to leave without Daddy.'

'This is all your fault.'

A small head appeared from the corner of our east-Mayo home. My sister's face was dark with soot.

'We'll get in trouble!'

'You are such a chicken. Do you want that fire to go out?'

My little sister was six: eight years younger than me. She wiped some dirt from her eyes and shook her head. We both knew it was the best bonfire ever seen in the townland of Lavey, Charlestown. Stacked the height of two cars, it was packed with whin bushes, old tyres, pieces of wood and whatever else the children of the area had been able to gather together over the previous two days.

Above Grainne's head I saw the black furling smoke rising thickly from the bottom field of our land into the twilight of the summer's evening. I heard the laughter and shouting of the others who were gathered below in the bottom field. Among them were our parents, who had yet to notice our disappearance.

'Why is it just us?' asked Grainne following my gaze.

'If too many of us leave, they'll notice.'

'Why us, though?'

'You were in charge of the petrol can.' She nodded, looking down at her feet.

'What did you put the whole thing on the fire for?'

'Joey told me to do it.'

'Humph.'

Grainne emerged fully from behind the house, her shoulders slumped.

'I'm sorry.'

'Then help me get more stuff. It's burning too quickly,' I said.

'OK.'

She was on board. I smiled. Secretly I was happy to be off on another mission. There was nothing I loved more than a mission.

'We never went to Ms Kilgannon's house,' I said, as I pushed the wheelbarrow down the driveway.

'She's in England.'

'She might have something just lying around.'

Grainne looked at me, her eyebrows rising. She hesitated.

'If it's rubbish we're doing her a favour,' I said, reading her mind.

'Mammy says we're not supposed to bother Ms Kilgannon. She's old.'

'We can't bother her if she's in England, now can we?'

Grainne still looked uncertain.

A few minutes later we arrived at Ms Kilgannon's grey and yellow home. There was no wall separating the back and front and the lawn stretched protectively around the walls of the house. With nothing of interest to be seen at the front, we made straight for the back.

It caught my eye the moment I rounded the corner. It was as if it was sitting there waiting for us in all its yellow glory. Propped inside the shed, just between the turf stack and the grey metal of the galvanised shed wall, its gleaming edges beckoned to us like the sweets in Junior Mulhearn's sweet shop. It was the answer to all our problems.

Grainne's eyes followed my gaze and widened.

'It's perfect,' I said.

Grainne nodded, a big smile on her face. It was a huge, thick wooden door that would surely burn for hours.

We dragged it from its resting place and pulled it on to the brown, rusted wheelbarrow. The clang made us both jump. We looked about us. Grainne's face was white. Had we attracted attention? We couldn't hear anyone. They were all at the bonfire.

'Run ahead and tell the others. Make sure Daddy isn't there,' I said to Grainne when we were back on the road again. It was a slow heavy walk back to our house but I gripped the handles of the wheelbarrow tightly and bit my upper lip.

'Gella, they are all inside,' said Grainne, meeting me at the top of our driveway. 'They're watching the news.' Brilliant, they wouldn't notice a thing.

As we made our way down towards the bottom field the others started to gather around us. Most of them were touching the shiny yellow surface, their eyes wide.

'Where'd you get that?' asked my sister Sinead, who was one year younger than me.

'Ms Kilgannon's,' said Grainne, smiling up at Sinead.

'You can't just burn someone's door.'

'It was out the back so she must be throwing it out,' I said.

'Daddy left me in charge of the bonfire,' said Sinead.

'But it's almost gone out,' I said. The others nodded.

Ignoring Sinead, I manoeuvred the wheelbarrow and its heavy burden towards the fire. The smell of burning rubber hung heavy in the air and I could feel it tickle the back of my throat. I set the wheelbarrow down carefully and rubbed my aching arms and wrists.

Moments later the gleaming yellow door crackled beneath

the heat of the flames that licked around it. We cheered in delight.

My father arrived some time later to wrap up the annual bonfire. He stopped dead and stared at the sight ahead of him.

'What in the name of God!' He pointed at the now blackened door. 'Where did ye get that?'

'Ms Kilgannon's shed,' replied Grainne proudly. I elbowed her so hard in the shoulder she squealed.

My father turned to me.

'Majella?'

I nodded slowly, dropping my eyes towards my toes.

'Is that fire still going?' asked Mrs Lavin, following my father into the field. Looking at my father's face she added, 'What's wrong, John?'

'They've just burned Mary Kilgannon's new front door.'

'The one you're putting up tomorrow?'

'Not now, I'm not,' he said, his face white.

A Healing Sting

Norman Fitzgerald, New York

'He had baggage, for one thing.' This is how my mother answers my enquiry about why her first cousin committed suicide. Our weekly telephone chat had been rolling along at its usual pace, with the usual questions and answers about health, the kids, my siblings and their respective marriages. I learned to stifle my yawns some years ago, having been caught out on too many occasions. 'Well, I suppose I'm not interesting enough for you,' she'd comment in a tone that was half-hurt and half-disappointment. We've damaged each other so much over the years with cruel and cutting words that she has become very sensitive to how I behave towards her, quickly retreating to a safe distance at the slightest hint of my desire to inflict pain.

The baggage comment catches my attention. My uninterested tone disappears. The yawning immediately ceases. Her son is present. Rattling along Route 184 in Connecticut, travelling at 80mph with the phone firmly to my ear, I keep pressing the volume up button in case I miss any of what is about to be offered. Information. Details at last.

When it happened, twenty-four years ago, little was said and less was asked. Eyes were immediately averted or the subject quickly changed at the slightest hint of an impending question about the untimely, self-inflicted death of Kevin H. Long. Angry Aunt Maureen's son. Hard-driving Maureen's eldest, over-achieving son. Bitter Maureen's Cambridge-educated, super-smart nuclear-physicist firstborn. Too smart. That's how

I saw it. Kevin H. Long had committed suicide because he was too intelligent to have the ability to make genuine human connections. Didn't have any real friends, had withdrawn to the safety of his research lab, was clearly too smart for his own good.

In the absence of real human connection, loneliness and depression crept up on him and one day they pushed him over a cliff on the Northern Irish coast on to the rocks below. I could picture his last moments: on his own, early in the morning, a clear, crisp day. He never hesitated. His slight figure, dressed in a suit and mac, went straight over and down to the rocks and the crashing, salty waves of the Irish Sea. He didn't so much jump off the cliff as continue his loping stride until there was no longer ground available to receive the soles of his patent-leather shoes.

Maureen's broken son had beaten her to the grave. The sight of the broken body of Kevin H. Long provoked an unmerciful wail from his mother, an emotional outburst of sorrow and pain that exceeded in its intensity all the feelings of love, appreciation and pride that judging Maureen had shown toward her son over his forty-seven accomplishing years.

In the absence of any real information that's what I made up.

'What do you mean "baggage"?' I ask.

'Well he saw something no child should ever see,' my mother answered, getting a little more engaged in the conversation herself. She knows when she has her son's undivided attention and she is going to take advantage of it.

'His father got drunk. Came home and raped his mother on the kitchen table in front of him.'

'Maureen?'

'Yes.'

'Grandpa Frank's sister?'

'Yes.'

'And Grandpa Frank knew this happened?'

'Of course.'

'Jesus.'

Silence.

'Christ, Ma, how long do I have to hang around before I get all the stories?'

She laughs, thrilling in the power she has over me. 'Well, while I'm at it, do you want to hear more about *that* family scandal?'

'What the bloody hell do you think?' I respond.

She laughs again, enjoying too the release she is experiencing from telling of the truth about her family's past.

'Before Maureen got married she was teaching at a private school in Northern Ireland. And she had, shall we say, a rather intense love affair with… My phone goes silent.

'With what, ma? Say it again. Ma, can you hear me? Goddammit.'

'She had a long affair with the headmistress before she met Kevin's father.'

Poor Kevin. Poor Maureen.

Under the Clock at Clery's

Maria Duffy, Lucan, Countu Dublin

Kathleen pulled her red, woollen coat up around her neck and shuffled in a little closer to her husband. O'Connell Street in Dublin's city centre was a hive of activity on a Saturday and standing outside Clery's, they were in the midst of it. She glanced up at the clock above her head. Almost four o'clock. Thank goodness. Maura would be along in a minute and they could escape this bitter cold. Maura was an old friend who was travelling to London to begin a new life. Sean had very generously offered to drive her to Dún Laoghaire where she'd board the boat to Holyhead.

To be in possession of a car in 1960 Ireland was more the exception than the rule. Sean was proud of his moonstone grey Morris Minor (affectionately known as Daisy) and loved to show it off whenever he had the opportunity. Today a gleaming Daisy had circled the city, depositing an enthusiastic Sean and Kathleen at various shops. Sean had recently won £134 on a newspaper crossword and they'd wanted to make a ripple in the small fortune. The prize should have been £500 but it had been split three ways. A reporter from the newspaper had arrived at the door of their little two-bed terraced house to break the news. He'd brought with him a photographer, who caused quite a stir with his rather conspicuous camera. Sean O'Malley would now be known around the neighbourhood not only as the man with the car, but the man in the paper – rich, clever and famous!

A dishevelled Maura eventually arrived under the clock, red-faced and breathless from lugging her suitcase half-way across the city. Luckily, in 1960, parking restrictions were practically non-existent and Daisy was patiently waiting at the kerb alongside her owners. After the customary greetings, the case was thrown into Daisy's rear and they were on their way.

Less than an hour after meeting Maura, Sean and Kathleen bade their farewell to her. Being seasoned travellers themselves and familiar with the lovely town of Dún Laoghaire, they decided to brave the elements and take a leisurely stroll. Kathleen loved how the salty air made her eyes water and filled her head with dreams of foreign shores. It was a world apart from the smog that hung over their inner-city abode.

It was going on for six o'clock when they arrived back at the car, noses streaming and ears screaming objection to the cutting breeze. Settling herself into her seat for the journey home, Kathleen took off her black leather gloves to reapply lipstick to wind-torn lips. It was then she noticed it and her heart began to race. Her engagement ring was gone. She quickly checked inside the glove she'd just taken off. Nothing. Oh God, what was she going to do? Her precious engagement ring. A mere five years of marriage and she'd already lost it.

Sean, having noticed her distress, took charge. There was no need to panic, he said. They spent the next half hour pulling poor Daisy apart. They searched behind seats, under mats and in every nook and cranny the car possessed. Nothing. With every minute that passed, Kathleen was becoming more and more frantic. Now there *was* a need to panic.

There was nothing else for it: they'd have to retrace their steps, paying particular attention to everywhere Kathleen had taken off her glove. They started back at the ferry port where they'd said goodbye to Maura, then the little coffee shop where they'd had tea and scones. Kathleen even went and checked in the ladies' room where she'd gone to fix her hair. Nothing. Sean tried to comfort her with promises of a new ring, but she wasn't interested. How could she ever replace her beautiful, precious engagement ring?

Despondency hung heavy in the air as they set off for home. But Sean wasn't ready to give up yet. With a new resolve, in a final attempt to find the ring, he suggested they go back to Clery's where they'd met Maura earlier. Kathleen didn't see the point but agreed that they might as well give it a try. They pulled Daisy up at the kerb at exactly the same spot where she had been parked only hours before. Kathleen sighed as she got out, the ever-darkening skies adding to her disillusionment. But Sean was already out of the car and kneeling down on the path. She'll never forget his words echoing in her ears: 'Well, I never...'

Clery's is a long-established department store on O'Connell Street in Dublin, a focal point of the street and the city. A large clock hangs above the central doors and 'under the clock at Clery's' was famous over the years as a place where romances began.

Sean and Kathleen, my Mum and Dad, are now almost fifty-six years married and I'm pleased to say that Mum still wears her precious engagement ring with pride.

How to Skin the Rabbit Man

Lawrence Cloake, Wexford

The following was told to me by my father, William Cloake, and I would like to dedicate the retelling of it to his memory.

There was great excitement around the village of Curracloe, especially amongst the lads of the local area. The hissing and puffing steam lorry, piloted by the rabbit man, had been heard negotiating the road from Blackwater and was, even now, turning into the field between the village and the church.

Coming up the road from the yallaclay lane were four young fellas: my father and his three brothers like Wyatt Earp, Doc Holliday, Virgil and Morgan Earp heading for the OK Corral. But instead of six-shooters bouncing on their hips they each had a brace of rabbits round their young shoulders.

Sixpence a rabbit.

And they had a plan.

Being the youngest, my father would execute the most dangerous part of their plan.

As they moved through the village toward the church, Dad slipped away into the graveyard and disappeared from view. My uncles, Patrick, Richard and Nicholas, continued on their way, following the other lads into the field.

The rabbit man had pulled his lorry across the field so that it was sideways on to them. He was standing beside the cab, his foot resting on the running board. He was a big man and as soon as he put all his weight on to the running board the lorry tilted alarmingly, enough for the young fellas in front to step back.

Once he was settled on the back of his lorry, he gave a sign for the first lads to start throwing their rabbits up to him. He had a knack of counting in the air, then catching the furry bundle and depositing it behind him with a flick of his wrist.

As their turns approached, my uncle Richard passed his rabbits to Nicholas. He then stood off to one side, close to the lorry, and waited.

Uncle Patrick threw the first and quickly followed with the second, but the third he gave a little extra push and watched as it slipped over the head of the rabbit man.

A moment later Uncle Richard felt a thump against his foot and bent down to retrieve the rabbit my father had thrown back under the lorry, having first caught it round the back. He waited for a short while and felt another thud against his foot. Then a nod from Uncle Patrick indicated that it was time for him to sidle back and slip the two rabbits to his brother.

That day they managed only two extra, but dad always maintained that there were days when they were so successful they were like kings walking back down the road, their pockets clinking with sixpence pieces and my grandmother saying to them that there weren't that many rabbits in the county, let alone that they would have the luck to catch so many.

If they had been caught, they probably would have ended up in the back of the lorry with the rabbits.

Miss Rochford

Gerry McDonnell

Miss Rochford worked for many years in Greene's bookshop in Dublin. She ran the upstairs second-hand department. She was kind to her customers, frequently sharing her morning break of tea and toast with a young poet. I was a regular customer and often I asked her to put aside some books for me, 'until Friday when I get paid,' I'd assure her. She'd put aside the small pile of books.

Sometimes, because of meeting debts in other bookshops around the city, it might be a fortnight or even a month before I'd call back to her. As I reached the top of the stairs, Miss Rochford would greet me across the room with, 'Mr McDonnell, Mr McDonnell, what do you think we are in here?' Browsers would turn, sensing my embarrassment. I would pay her contritely for the books and take the brown-paper parcel. Always, when I returned to the counter some moments later with more gems, she'd relent and set them aside also until, 'definitely next Friday, oh, absolutely.' Miss Rochford would take careful note.

The time eventually came for her to retire. She was given a surprise party in the shop one Friday evening. Staff and customers toasted her efficiency and her knowledge of books down through the years. You could see she was pleased. She announced that she looking forward to her retirement, to reading her own considerable collection of books in peace, in her garden flat in Monkstown. The following week, she was in the shop looking for her job back. She was very agitated. 'I can't stand not having a job to go to each day, not having my customers to look after,' she explained tearfully.

She was taken back and worked on for many more years, travelling to and from work on the Number 8 bus. One evening, at the terminus, the conductor was checking upstairs. To his surprise Miss Rochford was still on the bus. He went down to wake her, assuming she had fallen asleep, but found that she had passed away. 'She must have died somewhere on the route between Merrion Square and Dalkey,' he explained in the shop, a few days after her funeral. 'I didn't notice her,' he said, still shaken.

I never collected my final parcel of books from Greene's. They sat behind the counter, a monument to the generosity of Miss Rochford.

Dog, Lost

Fiona Tierney, Dublin

My sister was travelling on business for a couple of days and left her husband in charge of their three children and their dog. When she came back the children were all there but the dog was missing and had been missing for a least a day.

Her husband was not a bit worried, saying she would find her way home, but my sister was getting anxious when another day passed and still no sign of the dog. She called the local Gardai who informed her that a man had been in touch to say he had found a dog answering her dog's description (the dog's identification tag had long since gone). My sister was thrilled and made contact with the man to make arrangements to pick up her dog. He sounded a bit cold on the phone.

When she got to his house to collect the dog, he asked her how the dog had come to be lost. She said the dog had wandered off and thanked him most sincerely for keeping her and reporting her to the Gardai.

He then offered her the lead. 'Where did you get the lead,' she asked. The dog had been tied to the lamp post outside the local pub for a night and most of the next day. He knew this as he had seen the dog that evening and again the next afternoon still in the same place – which is when he stopped to untie her and bring her back to his house. My sister was lost for words (probably for the first time in her life) but made up for that when she got her hands on her husband!

The Pig-Killing Hat

Ronan Noone, Clifden, County Galway

The first place I visited after I left Ireland and went to America was New Orleans. It was always my intention to go there. I was in love with the music from a young age. Its culture fascinated me. It seemed to boast a pagan philosophy, a dark magic, which was in conflict with righteousness and the holy word. I liked to think it was a bit like myself. It was a purgatory, maybe, or a paradise lost. Of course it didn't matter whether any of this was true – all that mattered was that it was what I imagined. And out of this seemed to come mystery and creativity, things I was always looking for.

My first night there I got drunk in O'Flaherty's bar (closed now because of Katrina), which was owned by a fellow from Connemara. I wanted to ease into my adventure slowly. When I hit the right mindset I left O'Flaherty's and went to a casino on a steamship. I gambled at blackjack and listened to some Zydeco. I ate seafood gumbo. I heard some Louisiana creole. Outside, I was accosted by a guy who said for two dollars he could tell me where I got my shoes. Go ahead, I said. 'You got them in N'awlins,' he said. I took out my wallet and gave him two bucks. I didn't even think how foolish that was at the time. A few minutes later a woman asked me to take a picture of her and her husband. 'Of course,' I said. But then she asked me for my wallet so she could be sure I wouldn't run away with her camera. I gave her my wallet and I took the picture. She said thanks and gave me my wallet back. It was an adventure already but I wanted

The Pig-Killing Hat

something permanent, something that wouldn't let me forget my time there.

Next morning I woke up with a head like a bucket of frogs and I walked down by the promenade. There was a big gathering of tents, just like a fair day at home. I wandered in and out of them, picked up a souvenir, thought about buying it, and then I put it back, always the reserved Irish boy. I could hear my thrifty grandmother's practical advice: 'If you're going to spend money make sure you spend it on something you need and not something you don't need.' And then I stopped in front of a fellow who was selling hats. They looked like cowboy hats. They were all hanging off hooks on the roof of his tent. They were quality leather. I took one down. I put it on. I looked at it in the small mirror. I looked good. A long way from the bogs of Connemara. The owner was watching me but he wasn't bothering me, which was grand.

Being the furtive Irishman I am, I was just waiting to be put upon by some anxious salesman before I said, 'No, just looking,' and off I'd go. But this fellow stood back. Just watching me. Biding his time. He had half a dangerous look about him. A couple of earrings dangling from both ears and his black hair was matted to his head, the same as a wet runway. I respected the fact that he let me do my own exploring without pestering me. So I decided to ask him about the camouflage tanned cowboy hat I was wearing. And he said, as best as I can remember, 'That ain't no cowboy hat, sir. That's a pig-killing hat. See at the dark hour before the dawn when you leave the house on your hunt, the first thing you do is put on your pig-killing hat. You make your way into the fields. You find a single tree close to the centre of a field. You climb up that tree and you hold on tight to a strong sturdy limb and you wait. You wait till the sun comes sliding up over the horizon. And with your free hand you take some fresh, bright-yellow corn from your pocket and you drop it to the ground.

And those sensitive-smelling wild pigs, those with horns curling out from their jaws and jowls dripping with saliva, will make their way from the bush and gather around the tree to feed. Now this is danger time, sir. As the sun comes up you will see those fierce-looking creatures down below you feasting like pigs, if you will, and you know a wrong move from you and you could slip off that tree and a wild pig horn could slice through your jugular and your blood would pump out in life-ending spurts all over the tanned burnt grass and flecks of yellow corn. And you don't want that to happen, sir. No you don't. So you take your knife in hand. A good, sharp hunting knife with big, serrated edges, and you hold it out and as the sun brightens the spot under your tree you jump down on the back of one of those fat wild pigs and you slit its throat. And the reason you will be able to succeed in your endeavour, sir, is that the hat you're wearing will act as a deeeeskies. You understand? That pig-killing hat can save your life.'

Then he picked up a shiny black leather hat and he said, 'And this here is a true gentleman hat and you can't get one without the other, see, coz once you return home with that fine blood-soaked animal on your back, well, sir, you will need to swap hats. That way when you walk into town everyone will know you killed the pig. And of course it helps with the ladies too.'

I bought both those hats. And there's been many a pagan time since when I've found an excuse to wear them. Sometimes, I've even swapped them out on the same day.

Thoughts at the End of a Sunny Day

Regina Hennelly, Manulla, County Galway

It has been one of my better days, one in which tiredness did not kick in to any great extent, when my weight and blood pressure were normal and most of all, when an early inkling of summer weather lit up all that is good, casting my sad story into the shadows.

In the days after my diagnosis, I came to realise that crying for your fate becomes boring very quickly. Gradually, the sobbing comes to a reluctant and hiccoughing pause and you dry your tears and as the days pass and new medical words settle into your vocabulary, you notice that you are still carrying on with your life, albeit now in the grasp of unexpected, harsh circumstances.

There is something surreal about the adoption of such a new normality but it marks the point at which the mind and the body agree to an amicable separation. You learn to surrender and place your physical health in the hands of the medical brigade, cutting your body loose in a sense.

This is something you need to do, for your mental health. It won't happen immediately. In those initial stages you cling to the false notion we all live by, until some test results shatter the collective delusion that afflicts, or possibly protects all of human kind – that we are in control of our own destinies, that we can shape our future, eat right and work hard and succeed and live to be a great-grandparent.

That misconception disintegrates completely when your organs start to fail when you are in your twenties, which is the reality at the heart of my sad story. Both kidneys have given up and now there is dialysis and a wait for another chance at a full life with the donation of a new organ by a grieving family who will have just suffered their greatest loss.

Having surrendered the fate of my physical health to men and women of medicine, I look after the bit of me that remains the same, no matter how old I get, no matter how my body may break down.

I wake up on a glorious morning and respond as I always have, with the excitement of one who has a tree-house to build, or some such project to work on. I get up and go out. I eat ice-cream, although I shouldn't really. I run as fast as I can for as long as I can. I open all the windows and leave them ajar until night has fully fallen. Sleep comes a little more quickly, after a day of fresh air and sunshine.

Whatever the condition of my physical self, a day like this makes it somehow, blissfully irrelevant.

The Most Embarrassing Moment of My Life

Callum Spence, Dublin

'Cal, don't worry, you'll be fine. It's only fourths.' Only fourths? 'Just don't do something stupid like getting nutzed or…Ha! Remember against the YMCA in their tournament in sixth class, when you…'

Oh, I remember. My first hockey match for Monkstown, aged eleven. I remember being in a cold sweat putting my gear on, taking my helmet off repeatedly to wipe the sweat from my eyes. The unconquerable terror that gripped me as I stumbled, trance-like, to the goal.

The warm-up should have offered me some warning of the impending disaster. Alas, I saved everything that was to be expected of me and I pulled off a phenomenal piece of acrobatics to turn away a ball speeding to my bottom left. So, like a fox about to be roadkill, I confidently head-butted each post, the ritual bolstering my confidence further.

Such a change in the space of a bare hour is not uncommon in goal-keeping, but my ignorance of the storm on the horizon made me cocky. I challenged opposition players to enter my domain as kick-off neared. When we took to the pitch, I began beating my pads, the goalmouth and my helmet, creating such a din that my coach signalled me to stop. 'Ha! He won't care once I come off with a clean sheet!' Even now my recollection of such thoughts is perfect, a bulwark against future cockiness, perhaps.

My mother, anticipating my nervousness, flashed me a wide grin and gave me the thumbs-up. We kicked off and held possession for an obscene amount of time before YMCA even got a touch. They were dispossessed almost instantly. The attacks rained in on their goal and a score seemed imminent.

Meanwhile, I was growing bored. As anyone who does not play hockey will attest, it *is* boring, an overly tactical game that, unless certain schools from beyond the Pale are playing, is devoid of contact and action. For an eleven-year-old, this was a serious problem. Could I last the full game without at least taking a seat and releasing my burden of twenty pounds of gear? Encumbered as I was, I found myself getting tired despite minimal activity.

Then a solution presented itself, surely a divinely-inspired idea: I could sit on the backboard. Cushioned by my tailbone protector, propped up by the rigidly secure net, this seemed almost too good to be true. If only I had nourished that thought and let it trump all the others, but in my moment of weakness I opted for a more comfortable option and sealed my fate.

The previous day, I had been admiring my new Slazenger blood-red helmet (real blood the salesman had assured this gullible eleven-year-old), and had noticed how it had a wonderfully crafted protector for the back of my neck. This feature was added by the company because of the many complaints of the lack of protection from balls that rebounded from the net after a goal. Hardly necessary at U-12s but I still have the helmet and it's saved my skin numerous times.

Sitting on the backboard I assumed the air of a disinterested supporter and began to relax, slouching further back into the net. I remember thinking that I should buy a hammock, or rather instruct my financial controllers to do so.

The real test came when play broke and YMCA mounted an offensive against a bewildered Monkstown defence, which couldn't quite get over how the opposition had mustered the will to enter our half. Imperiously, I sat and predicted a fruitless end to their foray. When they came on further still into our twenty-five I got up, my presence inspiring my sweeper to pluck the ball from the attacker's stick and resume normal service.

Emboldened by this, I slumped back down and chided myself for not trusting my defence. But at that moment disaster reared its ugly head and blasted me back to Planet Earth. At the end of my slump my foot flicked off an indent across the goal line and I plummeted backwards. I attempted to get up but to no avail. My new neck protector had snagged on the net mesh and was refusing to budge.

As I struggled and squirmed, forcing my neck muscles into overtime, my dad spotted my predicament and came racing over as quick as a long-standing neck and back injury would allow. Instructing me to remain still, he began to work on the now heavily entwined knot.

Through the bottom of my visor, I saw a sight that chilled my blood: YMCA advancing with menace toward Monkstown's stranded keeper. Panic set in and with a rush of adrenaline I ripped my neck forward, snapping the neck guard off. Caught off balance by this sudden shift of weight, I staggered forward and out of position.

In such a crisis, I had two options, I could retreat and allow the attacker time to shoot but also time for myself to set properly, or I could charge him. With demonic fury I careered toward the attacker and launched myself at his feet.

Undecided whether to shoot or risk a one-on-one, he never stood a chance. I heard an audible wince from the spectators and a sigh of relief from the Monkstown collective and swatted the ball away to one of my heavily wheezing defenders.

While the umpire stopped play to investigate the extent of the poor child's injuries, I trudged back to the goal and resolved never again to seek to put my comfort ahead of duty as a goalkeeper. Now, my ability to see the warning signs has improved considerably and I have never again allowed myself to seek the relative comfort of the backboard. For a natural sloth, this has proved difficult at times, but when the urge to rest my weary legs becomes overwhelming I simply think back to that minute or so when, trapped in the back of the goal, I made deals with a more powerful entity to instigate a tectonic shift, swallow me into some great abyss or to immolate me in some freak lightning strike to my negatively charged helmet. Now, staring at my neck guard, I rip it along the line where it was dutifully repaired all those years ago and toss it into the bin. Coolly cantering to the goal and savagely head-butting each post, I think, 'What's the worst that could happen?'

And, if my instincts are as flawed as they were then, at least I will have material for further English essays, as long as prayers for deliverance go unheard.

The Guinness Man

Garret Pearse, Wicklow (by way of Longford)

As part of my college course, back in the early 1990s, I got to spend a year's work placement in Guinness's brewery. This was a time of change in the brewery, with many of the old work habits and practices dying out. There were still lots of stories of the old ways and the old characters floating around and this one was a particular favourite of mine.

The Guinness sales rep (the 'Guinness man') was expected to visit ten to twelve pubs in his area each day. It would have been poor form not to have a pint of the product with the landlord in each pub. This led to the reps keeping unsocial hours, not to mention unhealthy livers.

One such rep, Frank, was given to supplementing the Guinness with some whiskey, which he kept in a small glass bottle in the back pocket of his trousers.

Frank arrived home late from work one evening, the worse for wear after a long day of landlords, stout and whiskey. He staggered up to his front door, fumbling with his keys. He pushed the door key in a bit over zealously, sending him falling backwards on to his backside. His little bottle of whiskey shattered in his back pocket, shredding his poor posterior and leaving him with a very nasty, bloody cut.

An old hand, Frank quickly regrouped and crept quietly into the house, up the stairs and into the bathroom. He managed to clean up his cut with some tissues. Then, battling his drunken haze and the pain, he carefully placed two plasters over the wound by peering over his shoulder and using the bathroom mirror. He crept into the bedroom and slipped quietly into bed beside his long-suffering wife.

His wife awoke the next morning to find the sheets covered in blood. She frantically shook her husband to wake him up. 'Frank, Frank! You're covered in blood. What the hell happened to you last night?'

'Sh'all right, love,' Frank mumbled. 'Had a bit of a cut but I bandaged it all up. I'll be fine.'

His wife got out of bed and went into the bathroom. There, perfectly placed in the middle of the mirror, were two plasters.

The Last Visit

Martin Fitzgerald, Cork (now living in the Netherlands)

The same creak and clink from the whitewashed gate. The same weary apple tree seemingly held up by the swing hanging from it. The same smell in the small hallway.

As I was living abroad, every visit for the last few years had to be treated as if it might be the last. My grandmother, then well into her nineties, had started to slip away.

Her outspokenness, independence and, above all, her lethally dark humour were traits that made her wonderful company. By the time she reached her mid-nineties she had buried half her eight children. Watching her fading eyesight tormenting her and her mind failing her was uncomfortable.

My sister drove me to see her, warning me on the drive there that our grandmother hadn't been quite 'with it' in recent weeks. As was often the way, her front door was wide open and we walked straight into her kitchen. The sounds of our footsteps on the curling edges of the linoleum by the doorway were enough to announce our arrival and stir her from her doze.

Her eyes, visibly sore, half-blind and sleep-filled, squinted up at me as I stood over her. If she felt confusion she did her utmost not to betray it and she instructed me to sit down. I sat on the opposite side of the fireplace to her, while my sister, unnoticed, quietly took a seat by the door and lit her cigarette.

The conversation was the most uncomfortable that I had ever had with her, as her erratic mind pulled on the threads of the memories in her head, only occasionally letting her live in the present as she juggled with the realisation of who I was.

'Martin, Nana, living in Holland.'

'Ah, yeah, I know sure. You're in America now, aren't you?'

'No, Nana, Holland.'

'Ah, yeah.'

So it continued back and forth for an hour or more as dust flurried on the streams of weak afternoon sunlight all the way from the kitchen window to her slippered feet, as confused as the conversation.

I stayed chatting, trying to draw out the Nana I remembered, throwing frustrated looks at my sister behind her, who could only laugh between cigarettes. She'd been where I was many a time during my absence.

'Ah, Martin, I was always fierce fond of you,' she said, eyes closed, leaning back into her chair, adjusting the worn cushion behind the small of her back, pulling her navy cardigan across her chest.

'You're still up there,' she proudly announced, blindly pointing in the direction of the place on the mantelpiece where my First Holy Communion picture had been for more than twenty years, before being moved by a well-meaning friend or neighbour.

Believing she was having a semi-lucid moment I asked her what the doctor had said on his latest house call.

'I told the bastard I'd cut his throat if he sent me back to hospital.'

She did always like to be clear. I was still wobbling with laughter when she started talking about two of her sons, both long since passed away.

'And sure, Mikey and John don't call to see me any more.'

I looked nervously at my sister. 'How do you mean, Nana?' I asked.

'Mikey and John, your uncles, sure,' she replied, anxiously fingering the buttonhole on her cardigan, frustration evident in her voice. 'They never call any more.'

I didn't know what to say. Her mind was taking her back to a day only God knows how many years previous. Should I correct her? But what right had I to yank her memory back to the cold light of today when her sons were long dead and she couldn't see her hand in front of her face?

I looked to my sister for a hint; she shrugged her shoulders and drew deep on her cigarette.

'No,' she repeated and sighed. 'They never bother calling to me any more.'

While I hesitated, still unsure of how to break the silence, my grandmother leaned forward in her chair. She opened the one eye that hadn't yet completely failed her, turned to the fireplace and spat dryly into the embers, sending white ash into the air to settle on her slippers and my shoes, before turning again, half peering, half-squinting, to look directly at me.

'Although,' she said, 'that's 'cause they're fucking dead!'

As she threw back her head to laugh long and hard, we couldn't help but join in, on my last visit.

The Biscuit Tin

Des Cox, Dublin

In 2002, after three decades of growing up in Dalkey, County Dublin, I bought my own house in Rialto in Dublin's south-west inner city. This was an area I knew nothing about: my myopic understanding of Dublin just about extended to the stations along the DART line. I had chosen Rialto on the basis of first-time buyer affordability – in the pre-Celtic Tiger days, the red-brick terraced properties in this area of the South Circular Road were prized by bargain-hunters. I found my street on a map of Dublin, sandwiched between the flats of Dolphin's Barn and Fatima Mansions.

My mother was horrified and concerned for her precious son but my first lesson was how ignorance and prejudice can be very far from reality. My street and its residents are quite extraordinary and priceless. The terrace appears like a *Coronation Street* set: Number One: the married gay couple; Number Two: the student bedsit; Number Three: the single woman; Number Four: the African family. And me, the professional blow-in at Number Five. The rest of the terrace continues in this vein – the bachelor teacher, the single man-about-town, the bin man, the taxi-driver. And the Women, who position themselves with practised ease, leaning on the spiked railings surrounding the small front gardens, in order to engage in lengthy over-the-fence conversations. Neighbourhood Watch is not an option here, simply a fact of life.

And what kindness comes with neighbourliness. It is not forced, nor extended like a credit, with some suggestion that it should be reciprocated at some future point in time. It is genuine, taken for granted and more precious than fine gold. It is based on real interest in a person's life and welfare, not an intrusive nosiness. You are made to feel a part of the community and the street, when the Women invite you to sit with them outside their houses on a balmy summer's evening, sipping tea made by the Men and telling them about yourself, while they let you know who's who and what's what.

The general reason for the relative affordability of these properties was that they had often fallen into a serious state of dilapidation and required extensive rehabilitation. My house was no different. Mr and Mrs Daly, who had lived in the house for decades were, according to the Women (and, I'm sure, the Men, had they been allowed the opportunity to offer an opinion), just wonderful people; however, he was no builder, although that did not stop him carrying out all the DIY works in the house, including a rear extension, which had unfortunately collapsed by the time I put the key in the door for the first time as owner. In short, there was going to be a summer of hard labour ahead.

The dirt and dust as the house was being renovated were quite extraordinary. I was carrying out a great deal of the work myself, and as there was no running water in my house, I relied upon the kindness of herself in Number Three to provide the tea, missus in Number Four if I needed to use the toilet and yer wan in Number Twenty-One if I wanted a bath when I was finished for the night and heading into town. And woe betide me if herself in Number Three heard that I got a cup of tea from yer wan in Number Twenty-One, or if missus in Number Four noticed me heading to the toilet in another house.

It was in the midst of this chaos that I came across the biscuit tin. I had bought the house following the death of Mrs Daly, her husband having predeceased her by some years. Her children had, understandably, removed anything they wanted from the house, leaving it with a sort of pillaged look that matched its dilapidation. Curtains, utensils, even an old lady's wardrobe of clothes remained to be binned by the next owner. Of most apparent value was the Aga that filled the small kitchen. I had hoped to incorporate it into my renovated kitchen but a closer inspection found it to be beyond repair and it too had to be added to one of the many skips that landed outside the front door.

As I was heaving the heavy range out of the house, it toppled over and its heavy weight sent it crashing backwards on to the ground. The portion that connected to the chimney flue broke off and out of this space there fell a small, rectangular biscuit tin.

This was a totally unexpected discovery. Before commencing the renovation works, I had gone through the remaining contents of the house, finding nothing of worth or interest in what remained. But this biscuit tin? Closed and sealed, and clearly hidden by its owner. The decoration on the tin suggested it was old: maybe it had been placed in the range decades earlier, in the same way that valuables are placed in a bank vault. You hear about these people who keep their life savings in the mattress. Well, a biscuit tin in the old range seemed similar, the sort of thing you might expect in the inner city. Probably hiding the valuables from burglars or from the children.

What a dilemma. Since Mrs Daly's children had ransacked the house prior to my arrival, leaving me to dispose of the things they didn't want, did they really deserve to be recipients of her life savings, her jewellery or other valuables that might be contained in the hidden biscuit tin?

Or maybe the tin contained her will, leaving everything to the cats and dogs home: that could cause quite a legal dilemma. I decided to make the call as to whether to contact the children when I knew what the contents of the biscuit tin were.

With a feeling of nervous excitement I prised open the biscuit tin. At the very least, if there were photos inside, they would prove interesting to my neighbours and might allow me to get to know them better as we studied them over an evening cup of tea out on the road.

With the aid of a screwdriver, I finally opened the lid and peered in. Even I was unprepared for what I encountered.

Biscuits.

Long out of date, moulding. Not even decent biscuits, but cheap wheaten ones, no chocolate or icing.

Who the hell keeps biscuits for more than two decades after their use-by date, hidden in a secret compartment at the back of their cooker? Mrs Daly, for one.

I didn't trouble her children with my findings.

Eight years later, the house renovation is complete and my wife and child join me on a summer's evening, pottering in the small front garden, or leaning in a practised way on the railings, drinking a cup of tea or glass of wine with our neighbours and catching up with the weekly news.

The biscuit tin long since disappeared in one of those many skips, on to which it was thrown in disgust.

Pink Chiffon

Sheila Donohue, Cabinteely, County Dublin

Sunday night, 7.30pm, hair still in rollers and homework not yet finished.

But no matter what, by 8.30 she would be made up, hair back-combed, dressed in the latest and queuing with her friends outside the tennis club to dance the night away before catching the last bus home.

It was the oxygen that carried her through the week, just to dance and feel alive and get out of her school uniform.

Drugs had not yet arrived in Ireland, drink was not an issue as only old people went to the pubs and the lounge bar had not yet happened. So dancing was the drug that sustained the teenagers of the late 1950s and early 1960s.

A glance around the throbbing clubhouse as she emerged from the tiny cloakroom would tell her if the guy she fancied was there.

Oh, the guy who fancied her was sure to catch her eye. She never refused to dance with him but sometimes the smell from his breath would almost knock her over. Perhaps he was ill as he had a sickly pallor but he was always so polite she could never refuse that dance.

Then there was the guy who always asked her up for 'Pink Chiffon'. As soon as the first note of the tune rang out he was there in front of her – a nice guy. They both knew it was just 'their tune'. How it started neither could remember. She only knew his first name – Frank – and that was after eighteen months.

But the guy she fancied, the guy who hogged the bandstand

all night, the guy she had fancied for years, never gave her a second glance.

Tonight, she would ask him up for ladies' choice!

Knees almost knocking she crossed the twelve feet or so that separated them. She knew her voice quavered as she asked, 'May I have this dance, please?'

She knew immediately it was a mistake, as he reluctantly leaned away from the wall beside the small bandstand, took her hand and jived dutifully for the three tunes. Silence! She couldn't banter as she normally did when the first tune ended. How could she have read him so wrongly? No eye contact, nothing. At the end of the third tune: 'Thanks.'

She was amazed that an infatuation that had lasted years could vanish in ten minutes. Her heart felt like a stone sinking to the bottom of a cold, deep lake.

He returned to his post, she to her friends. 'Pink Chiffon' struck up. Frank appeared and happiness returned and they even went for a mineral. Frank was indeed a very nice guy.

A Sports Car and a Boyfriend

Fiona Cullinan, Enniskerry, County Wicklow

I had always wanted a sports car but it was a big aspiration as I was living on a student nurse's salary. But that is what banks are for. I persuaded the bank manager to give me a car loan and promised I would work all available overtime to repay the loan. My dad was a petrol head so he 'got' my desire and readily traipsed around garages with me – but to no avail. He made me promise not to buy a car before he checked it out, just in case it had been crashed.

However, one day I happened to be passing a garage in Rathmines and spotted this cool white sports car with bucket seats and alloy wheels, every girl's dream! In I went and I was greeted by a very handsome and very persuasive salesman. I had bought the car before I left the premises. I called my dad to tell him the good news and he was naturally concerned.

It was instant love. I loved everything about the car: the look, the sound of the engine, the wheels, the steering wheel – everything. What a great summer that was, with weekends spent zooming down the back roads of Dublin and Wicklow for the sheer fun of it.

Then winter arrived and so did the rain. After a twelve-hour shift at the hospital I went out to my car to drive home. I got into the car and took off, tearing down the straight road home to Rathmines from the hospital. But there are traffic lights on this route. As I approached one set, they turned from orange to red so I had to hit the brakes. I heard a noisy 'slushing' sound.

I looked down at my feet and where there should only be the pedals, there was a very significant quantity of water.

It transpired the car had been crashed. I could not afford to repair it so decided I would need to sell it. I was devastated. The advertisement went into *The Irish Times* and I got a call. I agreed to meet the potential buyer with my sister after a Saturday morning shift. He turned up, a charming, middle-aged gentleman dressed in a smart navy suit, white shirt, red tie. He said he was buying the car on behalf of his sister, who was at work in a large department store in town. The three of us drove around and he said he liked the car and made an offer. He dropped us back to the hospital, handed me a cheque for the asking price and drove off in my car.

I hopped on the bus and went out to see my boyfriend. I proudly told him I had sold the car and got the asking price. He advised me to put the cash away in a safe place. I explained I had got a cheque. He could not believe I had taken a cheque and admonished me for being so naïve. As I was working the following Monday he agreed to go to the bank and cash the cheque for me.

Monday came and it was a typical crazy day in the accident and emergency department. Just after lunchtime the senior nurse on duty called me to the telephone. I answered the phone to a detective inspector from Pearse Street Garda Station. He asked me if I knew a certain individual and named my boyfriend. He had arrested him in the bank for trying to cash a stolen cheque!

I burst into laughter with the image of my boyfriend being frogmarched out of the bank into a squad car! My boyfriend did not see the funny side of the situation. When I had verified the story my boyfriend had told the Gardaí the detective agreed to release him! I decided not to share my 'first sale' with my dad.

The detective inspector called me back and asked me to come into the station to look at photographs to see if I could identify the car thief. I did. He was an infamous con man. The Gardaí were confident they could track him down and get my car back. They did. They called me a couple of days later and asked me to come and collect the car. The con man had been unable to open the petrol tank and had done considerable damage by using a chisel to get the cap off. The spare alloy wheel was also missing. I now had a leaking car with a missing petrol cap and a significant repair bill.

Meanwhile my boyfriend, who had recovered from the shock of being arrested in a bank and who had not dumped me, was perplexed by the fact that the Gardaí had taken his fingerprints. He wanted the copy of his fingerprints back. I called the detective inspector, who agreed this would be possible. I could collect them from the station at my convenience.

A couple of hours later there was knock at the outpatient clinic where I was working. It was the detective inspector. He handed me an envelope. Twenty minutes later the phone in clinic rang and it was the detective inspector just checking I had the prints. Then he asked me out on a date!! I nicely explained that my boyfriend would probably not think this was such a good idea.

My boyfriend became my husband! We have been happily married for twenty-three years and have two gorgeous children. I now know that cash is king!

December's Work

Noeleen Kavanagh, County Wexford

Bruising or breaking were bad things. Then you could see the blood clots gather and pool below the skin, massive patches of purple. But the expertly twisted and broken necks were a good thing. The massive livid bruise on the neck and the head that flopped in time to the feathers being plucked meant that the job was being done properly. Among the pluckers there always had to be at least one man who was good at that.

They were hung upside down by their legs before they were killed. They struggled and flapped, their useless wings beating the air, trying to get away. Even when their necks were broken they still convulsed and jerked. Sometimes blood dripped from their beaks, bright-red drop by bright-red drop, to fall on the feathers below.

They took a long time to grow still in death. If they were not suspended they would damage themselves in their wilful refusal to die quietly. Birds with broken wings, with bruises or tears, sold for less, as who would want a mouthful of blood clots for their Christmas dinner?

The feathers floated down to layer on the straw and the turkeys hung, strung upside down. They were stripped naked to a pinkish-purplish colour by the pluckers. The big wing feathers were plucked first, while the turkey was still warm. If the turkey was left to grow cold, the big feathers were hard to pull out. The pluckers' hands were quick, a small, animal blizzard of feathers falling all around them. They talked and laughed as they worked.

Turkeys are ugly, stupid birds. They are big and a dirty yellowy-white colour. They make a stupid gabbling noise and they stink. Their heads look raw, incomplete, half-made.

That day they were hungry, not having been fed since the night before. Animals, unlike people, should be killed on empty stomachs. When the door into their house was opened they crowded away into a corner but after a few minutes surrounded you in their curiosity and hunger. They watched and gobbled as they were taken away two by two, carried upside-down from their house.

They spent their lives mostly in the dark. That day was the first time they were taken outside. Their first time in the watery December sunlight, under the washed-out December sky, was when they were carried upside down to their own slaughter.

Cut Up when Cold

Liz Macguire, Slieverue, County Kilkenny

Cut up when cold and pour over the custard: one of my favourite dishes, made by my grandmother and carried on for many years by my own mother. Bread-and-butter pudding is still a dish I search for, even in the finest of restaurants. In my grandmother's day it was a way of filling you up when supplies were very limited. Today it is probably considered 'a simple pudding'.

My grandmother lived with us until she passed away on Christmas Eve in 1967. I remember her for her beautiful white hair gathered neatly back in a little bun at the nape of her neck and covered in a silver net. She was a stern-looking woman with very set ideas, some would say a little above her station. She never understood the neighbours wandering in for a little gossip; she called it, with some venom in her tone, 'cabin hunting'.

Perhaps these attitudes stemmed from her own position in life. She worked as a housekeeper and when my grandfather's wife died and left him to rear two young daughters he employed her. They fell in love and married some time later. They had a son, Michael, my father, and, although times were hard my father spoke very warmly of this period in his life. He often told of stealing the bicycle of his stepsister, Kathleen, and speeding down bunkers hill as fast as he could go, stopping only when he landed on his knees in a gravel pit at the bottom.

They were probably better off than most people at that time as they kept chickens in the backyard and my father spoke of having an egg for his breakfast almost every day. My mother was not so well off, coming from a much larger family. She told us how she would pray on Good Friday that God would send them an egg for their breakfast on Easter Sunday – not even a chocolate one! As I got older I remember my stomach heaving as my father broke a raw egg into a cup and with one swift gulp, down it went without as much as a grimace. I never did take him up on his suggestion that it was good for your health. I think in fact my distaste for eggs probably stems from that very sight.

It was a time of much hardship but my father never complained at the lack of luxuries. Sorrow reared its ugly head only when he spoke of the death of his father and his stepsister Kathleen. Tuberculosis was rampant at that time and families were suffering all around him. He remembered coming home from school and hearing his sister coughing as he came into the street. Then his father began and it became part and parcel of the daily noises that surrounded them. In fact, he said, they took it in turns. First the chickens would start their clucking and then the coughing started, followed by bowls of warm water and lots of mopping of brows and cleaning of beds.

He cried every time he told the story of his father's death and that of his sister. In the church that cold November day the coffins stood side by side in silence. He missed the noise of coughing as its departure brought an eerie silence to the house in Mount Sion Avenue. He no longer had to steal the bicycle: Kathleen had called him to her room and with her last breath told him to go play on her bicycle. He said it was not so much fun any more, knowing that it was his at last.

'Cut up when cold' doesn't have the same meaning any more. I buy my bread now and, unlike my grandmother's home-baked loaf, I don't have to wait for it to go cold. I simply take it from the packet and layer it into a dish and follow her instructions. Perhaps it doesn't taste as good but I like it and I think it is a recipe that will pass down from generation to generation.

An Irish Waking

Caren Kennedy, Ringsend, Dublin

Exhausted from walking, he poured a single whiskey before leaning back in his chair and falling asleep. It was the quietness of him that disturbed his wife. The stillness and silence of him.

She touched his cheek for a moment, then feathered her fingers slowly down the creases of his neck, stopping only when she was sure nothing would disturb him again. Sighing, she reached for the phone. A few neighbours arrived, all expressing sorrow for her trouble.

'It comes to us all in the end,' she replied. 'He's at peace now, God love him. Ach, sure what a great way to go here in the warmth instead of out on the street.' She reached for the bottle that stood beside him and suggested a toast. 'Let's drink to long life and health beyond!'

The neighbours agreed that it's what he'd have wanted. 'We were due to go dancing this very night,' she said, filling glasses. 'He was seventy-two in age but not in mind.'

A good innings indeed, the growing crowd murmured. One neighbour recalled how he'd seen him earlier. 'Top of the morning,' I says to him, and would you credit it now his reply: "And the rest of the day to yourself!"'

Smiling, the wife sat down beside her husband. 'He took his walk every day, hail, rain or shine. He could surely have strolled to Dublin if he'd a mind to.'

'Have you phoned for the priest?' asked another neighbour.

'And the doctor too, much good it'll do him.'

She turned to her husband and, finding his eyes wide open, dropped her glass.

'Would you be in me grave as quick as in me whiskey, Missus?'

My Mother Wears a Car on the Third Finger of Her Left Hand

Jane Travers, Newbridge, County Kildare

At least, so I was always told as a child. As I had a vague notion that old cars were crushed and that diamonds resulted from the crushing of other substances, there was a strange logic to the story that I found perfectly acceptable. The true story was slightly different.

My father was never terribly demonstrative and his idea of a proposal was, 'When will we get married?' The purchase of the ring itself was a far grander gesture. A young captain in the Irish army, my father was about to be posted to Cyprus, with the knowledge that on his return he would be deployed to the border with Northern Ireland. Rather than leave my mother behind, he asked her to accompany him to Cyprus and marry him there. To this end he sold his prize possession, his first-ever car, an Austin A40.

In 1969, most officers of my father's rank would have spent one month's salary, or less, on an engagement ring. My father spent the equivalent of about three months', thanks to the sale of that car. Almost the entire proceeds went on the ring, a magnificent diamond cluster with a delicate gold band, almost too fine to hold the combined weight of the diamonds. It is a beautiful piece of jewellery, timelessly elegant and coveted by all who see it (including myself and my sisters).

Like any car, the ring has had its share of dings and dents over the years. When we were living in Israel in the 1980s, burglaries were rife and my mother put the ring on top of a wardrobe for safekeeping. Forgetting that it was there one day, she pulled a suitcase from the top of the same wardrobe, catching and dragging the poor ring till it was bent almost double. A few months later she left it behind in Jerusalem after a holiday, not missing it until we were home in Nahariya, several hours' drive north. The owners of the apartment we'd stayed in turned their home upside down and miraculously found it and returned it; it had slipped off my mother's finger while she was making a bed, and was stuck down the side of a mattress. (She left my little brother behind in the same apartment, but that's another story.)

On another memorable occasion, my mother replaced the ring on her finger after washing up, only to discover a stone missing. After turning the house upside down searching for the stone to no avail, she was so upset that she went to bed in the middle of the afternoon – something we children had never seen her do before, no matter how sick or tired she was.

This year my parents celebrated their ruby wedding anniversary, which means that my mother's ring, despite setbacks, has been going strong for forty years. I somehow doubt that my father would have got as much mileage out of that Austin A40.

The Human Spirit Is Alive and Well in Haiti

Mary Donohoe, Cork (Concern worker)

I am sitting in our team house in the hills on a Sunday morning, with the doors open and a cool breeze blowing, enjoying some time off after a very long and busy working week. The view over Port au Prince is stunning and it is very hard to believe that on the far side of the view are all the destruction, human misery and heartache that resulted from the earthquake that ripped Haiti apart earlier this year. On one side total destruction and on the other, life as normal. I am looking down on what is happening elsewhere. As I look to the right, in the distance I can see small white dots as more and more tents are erected and it is clear to me that the new settlement in the village of Taberre Isse is taking shape and is now almost ready for families to move into.

Concern Haiti has the responsibility for camp management at Taberre Isse, the first official location for the resettlement of people who were displaced from their homes by the earthquake. This settlement has been completed to a very high standard with the needs of the people identified and as much as possible provided for them. The delay in identifying locations for these resettlements is as a result of the whole issue of land rights in Haiti: it has been difficult for the government to find land they own or to persuade local landowners to lease back land to them.

More than five hundred families have now moved to Taberre Isse and they are beside themselves with excitement at having so much space to call their own. There is a feeling of real energy among the people here: they feel the need to take control and try to get life back to where it was before the earthquake. They also have the spirit of making the best of things, which in some of the conditions they have experienced since the earthquake is a real challenge. In Taberre Isse you see how remarkable the human spirit is. Families who arrived on the first day all come out to greet the new arrivals on days two and three and experience such joy when they recognise family members. On the days they arrive, Concern provides a hot cooked meal so they don't need to worry about food as they get themselves settled.

Already one family has put their pot plants in a line outside their tent. It is almost a statement: 'OK, if this is where I am going to live, my plants will come with me.' It is also funny to see people bringing their TVs and even a fridge into the tent, although there is no electricity to run these. But you can't blame them, as many have never lived in such a 'big' space. The instinct to create a 'home from home' is strong and, like the rest of us, all they want is a decent life for their families. In Haiti this is perhaps the biggest challenge of all.

The settlement has solar lights so safety for women and children is taken care of. We also provide water, rubbish collection and shower and latrine facilities.

The Concern team has worked with the host community so they don't feel they are being excluded, with all these 'strangers' being brought into their area. It is a delicate balance to meet everyone's needs in these first few days. As long as there is communication between the host community and the representatives of the resettled families in Taberre Isse there is hope and the Concern Haiti team is determined to help to make it all work. It is quite an inspiring place to visit: despite everything, children laugh and people smile and are filled with hope. This is a programme we in Concern Worldwide is really proud of.

INDEX OF AUTHORS

Brennan, Conal, 172
Brennan, Deirdre, 98
Brickley, Elizabeth, 88
Butler, John, 44
Cloake, Lawrence, 185
Collins, Jody, 29
Corduff, Ethel, 173
Cox, Alan, 166
Cox, Des, 204
Cox, Neville, 104
Crowley, Kathryn, 168
Cullinan, Fiona, 210
Daly, Liam, 144
Davis, Emer, 64
Delaney, Vanessa, 82
Deverell, Fiona, 128
Devlin, Barry, 93
Donohoe, Mary, 221
Donohue, Sheila, 208
Donohue, Siobhán, 47
Duff, Lyn, 150
Duffy, Maria, 182
Dunne, Mary, 72
Dunne, Thady, 108
Eklof, Cormac, 114
Fitzgerald, Martin, 201
Fitzgerald, Norman, 179
Fottrell, Quentin, 67
Gargan, Jim, 77
Gillett, Linda, 26
Hanrahan, Pat, 21
Hennelly, Regina, 193
Johnston, Fred, 124
Kavanagh, Noeleen, 213
Kennedy, Caren, 217
Lynch, Mary, 17

Mac Reannacháin, Pól, 74
Macguire, Liz, 215
McCombs, Mary, 137
McDevitt, Kathy, 153
McDonnell, Gerry, 187
Melia, Maura, 49
Mullen, Mary, 95
Ní Chonchúir, Nuala, 24
Noone, Ronan, 190
O'Beara, Clare, 90
O'Brien, Mary Clare, 60
O'Curry, Anne, 121
O'Donnell, Jack, 37
O'Dwyer, S., 160
O'Malley, Ian, 39
Owens, Michael, 15
Pearse, Garret, 199
Petter, Sylvia, 86
Piggott, John, 135
Purcell, Jerry, 170
Quinn-Einstein, Liz, 111
Reid, Majella, 175
Reidy, Paul, 33
Robertson, Sarah, 85
Scully, Barbara, 141
Sheehan, Mary, 56
Shiels, Andrew, 53
Smith, James, 31
Spence, Callum, 195
Tierney, Fiona, 189
Travers, Jane, 219
Troy, Adrienne, 157
Walsh, Eddie, 140
Walsh, Francesca, 148
Wells, Kevin, 118